The Missionary of Knowledge

Hastings Rashdall's Life and Thought

— CHRISTOPHER CUNLIFFE —

Sacristy Press

Sacristy Press
PO Box 612, Durham, DH1 9HT

www.sacristy.co.uk

First published in 2024 by Sacristy Press, Durham

Copyright © Christopher Cunliffe 2024
The moral rights of the author have been asserted.

All rights reserved, no part of this publication may be reproduced or transmitted in any form or by any means, electronic, mechanical photocopying, documentary, film or in any other format without prior written permission of the publisher.

Every reasonable effort has been made to trace the copyright holders of material reproduced in this book, but if any have been inadvertently overlooked the publisher would be glad to hear from them.

Sacristy Limited, registered in England & Wales, number 7565667

British Library Cataloguing-in-Publication Data
A catalogue record for the book is available from the British Library

ISBN 978-1-78959-334-1

For Helen

Contents

Preface and acknowledgements v
Abbreviations vii

Introduction 1

Chapter 1. Rashdall's life and character 6
Chapter 2. Dean of Carlisle 24
Chapter 3. Rashdall the historian 33
Chapter 4. Rashdall the philosopher 46
Chapter 5. Rashdall the theologian 63
Chapter 6. Pursuing good and resisting evil: Rashdall's theology
  in practice 85
Chapter 7. Rashdall's legacy 110

Select bibliography of Rashdall's works 123
Index 125

Preface and acknowledgements

My interest in Rashdall began as curiosity and slowly developed into a desire to rescue his thinking from what I considered to be undeserved neglect. I came at him from two directions. The first was through academic work on the historical context of two representatives of the tradition of British moral philosophy, the third earl of Shaftesbury and Bishop Joseph Butler. I saw in Rashdall a later representative of that tradition: he made frequent references to Shaftesbury in his writings and lectures, and intended to write a book about Butler, although the pressure of other commitments forced him to hand the task to someone else. My second encounter with him was as a student of theology, while training for ordained ministry in the Church of England and, subsequently, exercising that ministry. Like most clergy, I was faced with the challenge of articulating the Christian faith in the contemporary world, in a way which was both spiritually enriching and intellectually serious. Rashdall's was a name which cropped up from time to time, and I was attracted by the liberal, modernist outlook which he and others represented, whether in my own Church or elsewhere. That impression has become more nuanced over time, but it has not faded, which is why I have written this book as a way of crystallizing this stage of my exploration.

Over the intervening years, other things have taken centre stage, but Rashdall has been there in the background and my ideas about him have been marinating. Specific opportunities have presented themselves along the way. A period of study leave in 2011, taken with the encouragement of the Bishop of Derby, Alastair Redfern, enabled me to make a brief initial foray into the voluminous Rashdall papers held in Oxford, at New College, the Bodleian Library, and Pusey House. Then, in Michaelmas Term 2017, I was privileged to be awarded a Farmington Fellowship at Harris Manchester College in Oxford. I must thank the Principal, Ralph Waller, and Fellows for giving me the opportunity to be part of

v

such a congenial and intelligently supportive society, which enabled me to start writing the draft of this book and to do further work in the archives. That thanks extends to other members of Harris Manchester for their help and to the staff of other institutions: New College, Oxford, the Bodleian Library, Pusey House, Oxford, and Harrow School, who have been welcoming and accommodating in providing manuscripts and following up leads.

Quotations from papers held in their archives appear with the permission of the Warden & Scholars of New College, Oxford.

My particular thanks are due to Adrian Botwright and Alastair Redfern, for reading a complete draft of the text and offering helpful advice, gentle warning, and welcome encouragement. Draft chapters benefitted from the scrutiny of Michael Brierley, Jake Cunliffe, Bill Mander, and John White, while Alice Lampard and Nadine Waldron commented on earlier drafts. Jane Garnett, Tom Hurka, Alastair Land, Erica Longfellow, and Amia Srinivasan were generous in their assistance with specific questions. I am also grateful to Natalie Watson and her colleagues at Sacristy Press for their expertise and patience in bringing this project to a conclusion.

Books are not written in a vacuum. Over what must have seemed to them a very long time, my wife, Helen, and our sons, Edd and Jake, together with their families, have created the environment which allowed this book to be completed. Its dedication to Helen, who, as a theology undergraduate at Oxford, probably came across Rashdall earlier than I did, is a small token of my love and gratitude.

Christopher Cunliffe
Llandeilo, Carmarthenshire
July 2023

Abbreviations

The following is a list of sources which occur frequently in the footnotes.

Manuscript Sources

Bodl. Lib., Add. MSS.	Bodleian Library, Oxford, Additional MSS.
Bodl. Lib., R. H.	Bodleian Library, Oxford, Ripon Hall MSS.
New Coll.	New College Archives, Oxford
Pusey H.	Pusey House Library, Oxford

Printed Sources

D and D	Doctrine and Development
Idea	The Idea of Atonement in Christian Theology
JH	John Huss
TGE	The Theory of Good and Evil
Universities	The Universities of Europe in the Middle Ages
Matheson	P. E. Matheson, The Life of Hastings Rashdall D. D.
ODNB	Oxford Dictionary of National Biography

Introduction

This book is not a complete biography of Hastings Rashdall, although it is written from the conviction that knowledge of personal and historical context is essential to understanding the significance and impact of someone's ideas. Nor is it a comprehensive survey and assessment of his thought, although it sketches its main outlines. Rather, it is intended to be an introduction to the life and thinking of one of the most significant figures in the Anglican theological world of his time, whose contribution deserves to be revisited as it still has much to say to those dealing with similar challenges a hundred years later.

The book's starting point is a sermon which Rashdall preached in 1921, towards the end of his life, in which he revisited a theme he had first articulated in his thirties, and which he revisited throughout his career. In "The Greatest Need of the Church", Rashdall surveyed the challenges facing the Church of England in the aftermath of the First World War and was convinced that its relationship with the intellectual life of the nation was in most need of repair. He wrote:

> A church that has lost its hold over the intellect of the age will not long retain its hold over its emotional life or its practical activities.[1]

A hundred years later, few people would argue that the trend which Rashdall identified has not continued and deepened or that the remedies he suggested—improved training for the clergy and greater intellectual engagement with their faith by laypeople—would now be an adequate response. Yet the need for a coherent statement of the Christian faith which is intellectually convincing as well as religiously satisfying is as

---

[1] *God and Man*, p. 257.

urgent as ever. The task is a daunting one, but a study of the thought of someone who took seriously the articulation of the Christian faith in dialogue with the best philosophical, historical, and scientific thought of his time, and who wished to relate it to a rapidly changing social, economic, and political environment, may be of some benefit to those attempting a similar venture in the first half of the twenty-first century. Times have changed, and it would be fruitless to expect Rashdall's answers to be ours. Indeed, George Newlands was to comment on the remoteness of earlier theological preoccupations: "By 1976 things had changed: the God of Hastings Rashdall was as remote as the God of Cyril of Alexandria."[2] As Rashdall himself wrote of an earlier apologist, Bishop Butler: "It is scarcely possible to exaggerate the obsoleteness of Butler in many ways . . ."[3] Rashdall's approach, however, his wide-ranging knowledge and sympathy, as well as his impatience with lazy and inaccurate thinking, has much more to offer than mere historical interest.

Not only was Rashdall a deep and influential thinker. In his busy life (one wonders whether Rashdall was ever still in a profound way), he was always eager to put thought into action, whether by way of the Church's critical engagement with the social and economic problems of late-Victorian society, involvement in matters of university reform or the governance of the Church of England, teaching adult education classes for railway workers in Carlisle, or simply helping people to live better and more examined lives, by spending time to help individuals as they faced difficult decisions. A letter from William Temple, later Archbishop of Canterbury, may stand as an example of this last aspect of Rashdall's ministry:

> Being here [Oxford] I feel specially conscious of all your help to me when I was an undergraduate, both on our delightful walks and at other times—help which I continued to receive until I

---

[2] George Newlands, "Cambridge: As a Theologian", in C. F. D. Moule (ed.), *G. W. H. Lampe: Christian, Scholar, Churchman: A Memoir by Friends* (London and Oxford: Mowbray, 1982), pp. 59–60. Lampe himself would have made a more positive assessment of Rashdall's contribution.

[3] *God and Man*, p. 231.

left Oxford for Repton. If we did not then always agree and have not always done so since, I am often aware of wider sympathies than would have been possible to me apart from your influence. And I know that at a rather critical time in my life that influence, rooted in your combined love of truth and personal devotion to our Lord, was of supreme value.[4]

Any study, especially a brief one, of a person's life and thought, particularly of one so prolific and wide-ranging as Rashdall, is bound to risk imposing too rigid a structure on the complex interplay of ideas and relationships which constitute the life of a public intellectual. In Rashdall's case, however, the three major strands in his thinking coincide chronologically with the three major published works with which he is associated. The first is his early work as an historian, encapsulated in his *Universities of Europe in the Middle Ages* (1895). Secondly, there is his work as a philosopher, and especially a moral philosopher, in *The Theory of Good and Evil* (1907). Finally, his more specifically theological output, of which *The Idea of Atonement in Christian Theology* (1919) is the outstanding example. This is not to say that Rashdall's life was compartmentalized—he wrote on theology early in his career and was revising his history of the universities at the end of his life—but these major publications inevitably provided a focus of energy and attention at particular times of his life.

---

[4] Temple to Rashdall, 22 May 1923, cited in Matheson, p. 223. Percy Matheson, as a Fellow of New College, Oxford, was a colleague of Rashdall's and was asked by his widow to write the authorized biography. He thus had early use of the extensive Rashdall papers donated to the college archives and the Bodleian Library, as well as easy access to Rashdall's friends and colleagues. Matheson's work stands as a tribute by an admirer. For a helpful, much briefer account, see Jane Garnett, "Rashdall, Hastings (1858–1924)", in *Oxford Dictionary of National Biography* (Oxford: Oxford University Press, 2004), vol. 46, pp. 72–4. Rashdall also features as the subject of a chapter, rather quirkily entitled "The Theo-Philosopher of Carlisle", in David Baggett and Jerry L. Walls's more recent book, *The Moral Argument: A History* (Oxford: Oxford University Press, 2019), pp. 97–113.

To consideration of his published work should be added his role as a public theologian. It might fairly be said that Rashdall was a keen polemicist in what he saw as the service of the truth. He believed that there was one truth, and he was pugnacious in his attacks on those he perceived as straying from it or proposing implausible alternatives. This is not to say that he had a fixed idea of what that truth is, as he was a strong believer in the idea of development, that we can know the truth objectively but not (yet) ultimately. He wrote to a correspondent in 1920:

> Is not the whole development of Christian thought a gradual progress towards the truth? Is not this really implied in the doctrine of the Holy Spirit?[5]

Rashdall's combative approach was commented on by the Oxford philosopher, H. A. Prichard, who had succeeded him as philosophy tutor at Hertford College:

> There was a forcibleness and earnestness about what he said which compelled attention; and whether you agreed with him or not—and very likely you did not—you realized at once that these qualities would produce an effect, even if sometimes it took the form of a reaction.... [I]n what may be called his public life, [he was] first and foremost a fighter who delighted above all things in being the champion of causes which he thought unpopular but important.... In many ways he irresistibly reminded me of Dr Johnson, whom he was never tired of quoting. And though there was a large element of pugnacity about him—no one could deny that he enjoyed a "scrap" and even treading on the toes of those from whom he differed—there was much more than pugnacity behind the vehemence and directness with which he pressed his views—chiefly, I think, intense religious and moral conviction and great moral courage.[6]

---

[5] New Coll., PA/RAS/6/2, Rashdall to Feltoe, 16 March 1920.
[6] H. A. P[richard]., "Dr. Hastings Rashdall", *Hertford College Magazine* 13 (April 1924), p. 6.

Although he was fierce in his polemic, although he was himself sensitive to criticism and attack, Rashdall was motivated by the love of truth and a hatred of injustice; he took seriously his place in the ranks of those fighting in the battle for good against evil. His close Oxford colleague, H. W. B. Joseph, who was himself a forbidding presence to his pupils, wrote of him after his death:

> *Impiger* [energetic], *iracundus* [irascible] he was, and *acer* [keen]; but save in points of principle, never *inexorabilis* [relentless]; and he leaves behind him the memory of a powerful mind consistently devoted to high and worthy ends, and of a most lovable personality.[7]

---

[7] Matheson, p. 254.

1
Rashdall's life and character

In its outward form, Rashdall's life was conventional and unremarkable. Born to a clerical household in London in 1858, he was educated at Harrow School and New College, Oxford. After a brief excursion to Wales, as a tutor at St David's College, Lampeter, he moved to Durham for five years, to University College, during which time he was ordained. Then, in 1889, back to Oxford for the central part of his career, first as a Fellow of Hertford College, followed by a return to New College in 1895. He stayed there for 22 years, getting married in 1905, and holding his college post in conjunction with a residentiary canonry at Hereford Cathedral from 1910. Finally, in 1917, came his appointment by Lloyd George as Dean of Carlisle, where he stayed until his death in 1924.

To reduce Rashdall's life to such a bald summary, however, hardly does justice to him; nor does it explain the inescapable connections between his life and his work. Rashdall wrote powerfully about the individual as a moral agent, and their knowledge, feelings, and will. His presuppositions, motivations, prejudices, anxieties—what made him tick—are always apparent in this most engaged of thinkers and writers. To understand his thought better, it is important to take account of his formation and development as a person.

The world into which Rashdall was born was the conventional and comfortable society of middle-class mid-Victorian England. The country was flexing its muscles as an international and imperial power: the Crimean War had ended in 1856 and the Indian Mutiny was suppressed in the year of his birth. The following year, 1859, was notable in literature for the publication of Dickens's *A Tale of Two Cities* and George Eliot's *Adam Bede*, as well as the appearance of Charles Darwin's *The Origin of Species*.

Rashdall's father, the Revd John Rashdall, came from a Lincolnshire family. As a young man he struck up a friendship with the poet Tennyson, who was a near neighbour. The friendship continued after John Rashdall's ordination and his subsequent move away from Lincolnshire. Hastings Rashdall was to write of Tennyson, together with Browning, as being the great "poet-theologians" of the nineteenth century. In 1857, John Rashdall married Emily Hankey and moved to London to minister to the fashionable congregation at the Eaton Chapel in Belgravia, founded in 1836 as one of a number of chapels in the old parish of St George's, Hanover Square, and demolished after its closure in 1901. The Hankeys were a banking family with significant evangelical connections, to the Clapham Sect as well as more broadly. Rashdall's aunt, Kate Hankey, a near neighbour in London, wrote the famous hymn, "Tell me the old, old story". It was at his parents' new house in Kensington that their first child, Hastings, was born on 24 June 1858, and named after his paternal grandmother's brother, Hastings Bonner. There were to be two more children—Edward Montagu (Monty), who was born in 1860 and died at the age of 28, and Agnes (Aggie), born in 1862.

The Rashdall family was, by all accounts, a close one and there was also close contact with various members of the Hankey family. When Rashdall was six, his father became vicar of Dawlish in Devon. Five years later, in 1869, John Rashdall died at the age of 59. His diaries and correspondence reveal a widely read and well-travelled man, well connected in the literary world. Morally serious, without being puritanical, and prone to anxiety and depression, John Rashdall combined firm churchmanship of an evangelical character with a love of well-ordered worship. His breadth of sympathy led him to work closely with dissenters, a foretaste of his son's later ecumenical endeavours.[1]

Rashdall's mother was a dominant, perhaps the dominant, figure in his life. Emily Rashdall was a well-read, highly intelligent woman, who took an interest in theology and church affairs. Rashdall's widow, Connie, remembered her as "naturally gay and liking to wear her 'pomp' as she

---

[1] See Matheson, pp. 1–4, for an outline of John Rashdall's life and family background. John Rashdall's journals, donated by Constance Rashdall, are at Bodl. Lib., MSS. Eng. Misc. e. 351–60.

called her pendant, [she] never once went to the theatre, though she recognized how changed it was, as it would 'spoil a long life', but never objected to any of the family going. [She] must have been over 70 when I first knew her and she was widowed at 37 and lived to 92, she never wore anything but black bombazine and kneedeep crepe."² At the time of his mother's death, Rashdall wrote to Clement Webb, an Oxford colleague and friend, that "she retained the full clearness of mind and memory till she had about a month ago a fall in her bedroom which a few days later brought on periods of delirium . . . . She had always had a great dread of becoming 'dotty.'"³

Emily Rashdall died in 1923, the year before her elder son. There remain in the archives at New College nearly 600 letters which Rashdall wrote to her over a 56-year period from 1867, when he was nine, to 1923, all in their original envelopes and all in his atrocious handwriting. That she kept this correspondence so carefully preserved is a sign of the bond between them. Much in a correspondence of this nature is bound to be quotidian and ephemeral—a request for more nightshirts; an enquiry whether he has left his ice-axe at her house after a climbing holiday in Switzerland—but it also contains evidence of Rashdall's theological outlook and his views on current affairs. His letters to his mother provide the connecting thread for Percy Matheson's 1928 biography and are indispensable to constructing a narrative of Rashdall's life. They also raise the question whether he entirely shook off the sense of emotional dependency on his mother and on other quasi-parental figures such as Montagu Butler, his headmaster at Harrow. Might the pugnacious and polemical behaviour of the later public figure have had its roots in a nagging insecurity?

Rashdall's sister, Aggie, was also long-lived, dying in 1956 when she was in her nineties. After her brother's death she wrote some reminiscences of his early life to help Matheson with that part of his biography. Her own memories were augmented by conversations with her mother, with whom

---

² Bodl. Lib., MS. Eng. Misc. c. 590, fol. 2r, Constance Rashdall to J. N. L. Myres, 31 March 1953.
³ New Coll., PA/RAS, 6/2, Rashdall to C. C. J. Webb, 2 June 1923.

she lived for much of her life. This affectionately perceptive portrait reveals character traits which were present at an early stage:

> Hastings was very like [his mother] in natural conscientiousness and sense of duty—especially in what I can only express as the sense of duty to the community, "doing one's bit". I think it was that quality which gave us younger ones a very real under-lying respect for him & reliance on him—though I am afraid we teased him a great deal. He was naturally a rather irresistible person to chaff, with his entire incapacity for anything in the shape of a game, & his curious vagueness in all the little details of everyday life.[4]

She also commented:

> But I never remember him being the least bit of a prig (& brothers & sisters are pretty keen critics!). He was entirely devoid of self-consciousness, & I don't think it ever occurred to him to consider what people thought of him.[5]

Agnes Rashdall's account is also the source of a number of childhood stories, particularly to do with his interest in liturgy and ceremonial, where he was influenced by the high-church inclinations of one of his father's curates. They include the story of Rashdall preaching to his brother and sister in the nursery, wearing a nightshirt for a surplice and a red stocking for a hood. But his enthusiasm was not confined to the home. On one occasion Rashdall went with his nurse to a weekday service at one of the daughter churches in the parish in Dawlish, when there was a churching, a short thanksgiving after childbirth, which was a common occurrence then:

---

[4] Bodl. Lib., MS. Eng. Misc. c. 590, Notes for use in the Life of Hastings Rashdall n.d. (1925?), fols 116–17.
[5] *loc. cit.*, fol. 108.

> .... [B]y some accident the clerk did not appear—before he could be stopped Hastings slipped out of his seat, knelt down by the woman, & repeated all the responses in a loud voice! When my Mother afterwards tried to explain to him that it was not his business he only answered, "There was no-one else".[6]

"There was no-one else" and "doing one's bit" became important themes in Rashdall's later understanding of life as a vocation.

Agnes Rashdall remained more committed to the evangelical character of her family upbringing and noted her brother's divergence from it, in a shrewd comment:

> Nevertheless, Hastings was never attracted by Evangelicalism, & I rather felt myself that he never understood its spirit (as apart from its formal theology), & was not always quite fair to it.[7]

———

Rashdall was eleven when his father died. His mother moved the family to Cheltenham and turned her attention to her eldest child's education. Taught at home until the age of eight, Rashdall had attended small private schools in Dawlish and Dartmouth, and a similar establishment in Cheltenham. The question which taxed his family was which public school he should move to. Despite winning a scholarship to Cheltenham College, the final choice was Harrow School, which he entered in September 1871. The decision was to prove a momentous one for the slightly odd, intensely serious boy. It has become fashionable to mock the deficiencies of the traditional English public-school education and draw attention to its unthinking prejudices and the opportunities for physical and emotional abuse. For many, it was an unnatural environment, taking them away from their families and their local connections for large parts of the year and exposing them to the misunderstandings and occasional cruelties of their peers. For some, however, including some

---

[6] *Ibid.*, fol. 105.

[7] *Loc. cit,*

of the more reflective and introspective, it provided an opportunity, through close contact with sympathetic and inspiring teachers and fellow pupils, to create a way of life and thought which was hugely positive and informative, both intellectually and emotionally. Both Randall Davidson and Charles Gore, for example, a future archbishop and bishop respectively, benefitted greatly from their encounter at Harrow with B. F. Westcott, the New Testament scholar and future Bishop of Durham, who was on the teaching staff for nearly 20 years. Such was Rashdall's experience of Harrow. The principal attraction of the school was its growing reputation under the headmastership of Montagu Butler. Butler, himself the son of a previous headmaster, had taken over the school in 1859 in difficult circumstances, following the hurried resignation of C. J. Vaughan, reputedly under the threat of blackmail over a homosexual affair with a senior pupil.[8] This was a time when the older public schools were undergoing a period of reinvigoration and reform, associated particularly with the name of Thomas Arnold, headmaster of Rugby School, and codified in legislation during the 1860s, as a result of the work of the Clarendon Commission of 1861-4. Vaughan had himself been a pupil of Arnold's at Rugby and, when he moved to Harrow, increased the size and popularity of the school considerably. Butler built on this foundation, literally so in the construction of new facilities, but also in the broadening of the curriculum, in effect creating a modern school during his 25 years in the post. The historian of Harrow School, Christopher Tyerman, wrote that "Butler presided over one of the great powerhouses of the late nineteenth-century British Establishment during a Head Mastership that defined Harrow's reputation, character, and standing."[9]

It was into this environment, and into Butler's own boarding-house, that the fatherless young Rashdall moved, and found in his headmaster a sympathetic and supportive presence, as well as an exacting teacher.

---

[8] For a clear and balanced account of the complexities of the Vaughan affair and the shock caused by his precipitate resignation, see Christopher Tyerman, *A History of Harrow School* (Oxford: Oxford University Press, 2000), pp. 275–83.

[9] Tyerman, *A History of Harrow School*, p. 303. Butler's regime and his influence on the school is described in greater detail at pp. 303–54.

Agnes Rashdall recalled that "Dr Butler became his best friend & one of the strongest influences in his life." She went on to write:

> ... just after he was 17 he became head of Dr Butler's large house—the position would have been a difficult one if it had not been for Dr Butler's continual help and support—my Mother has told me how he used to finish his nightly round of the house by coming into Hastings' room to sit over the fire with him & encourage him to talk out all his difficulties.[10]

The "dear man", as Butler was known in the Rashdall family,[11] kept a close watch on his charge, exercising that "tenderness and sympathy towards a fatherless boy" which Rashdall's widow thought worthy of mention some 80 years later.[12] Butler and his wife kept the anxious mother informed of progress:

> His mental growth seems to me most healthy—his constant forgetfulness most amusing—his writing, blots, erasures &c abominable.[13]

---

[10] Bodl. Lib., *op. cit.*, fol. 111. During Rashdall's time as head of house, there was an incident, clearly reflective of a more prevalent ethos, which led to the expulsion of a number of boys, giving him an early experience of the challenges of institutional leadership. He wrote to his mother about an episode of "gross immorality" in the house, resulting in the expulsion of seven boys. (New Coll., PA/RAS, Box 4/1, Rashdall to E. M. Rashdall, 22 February 1876; see also same to same, 31 March 1876.) Another significant influence on Rashdall at this time was the classics teacher and strong Liberal in politics E. M. Young, later headmaster of Sherborne. For him, see Tyerman, *A History of Harrow School*, pp. 317–18, 330, 360.

[11] Bodl. Lib., *op. cit.*, fol. 112.

[12] Bodl. Lib., MS. Eng. misc. c. 590, fol. 1r, Constance Rashdall to J. N. L. Myres, 31 March 1953.

[13] Bodl. Lib., MS. Eng. lett. d. 353, fol. 57v, H. M. Butler to Mrs Rashdall, 3 November 1875. A Harrow contemporary remembered that "H. R. was not infrequently put back from early School by the Head Master to brush his

The two maintained their easy relationship until Butler's death in 1918 as Master of Trinity College, Cambridge, where he moved in 1886, and where Rashdall was a frequent and welcome visitor at the Master's Lodge. In dedicating his volume of sermons, *Doctrine and Development*, to him in 1898, Rashdall called Butler "my earliest theological teacher", and it was the Bible which Butler gave to the Rashdalls as a wedding present that they used for household prayers.[14] Rashdall's biographer recounts that Dr Butler, when asked whom he considered his most distinguished pupil, replied, "It is not easy to say, but if you press me, I think—Rashdall."[15] And this from the headmaster of Randall Davidson, Charles Gore, and Stanley Baldwin, among many other distinguished pupils.

What did Butler see in Rashdall? It was certainly not the exact scholarship of the kind required to excel in the study of Latin and Greek literature, and of which Butler himself was a master. Latin and Greek composition, verse, and prose were always Rashdall's weak point. Yet, with the encouragement of his teachers, he read widely in other subjects, from theology and history to geology, winning school prizes and making an impression both inside and outside the school, becoming known as its best speaker and debater. Charles Vaughan, Butler's predecessor, wrote to a friend about a visit to the Harrow speech day in 1875: "I heard the speeches, & was struck by the cleverness of young Rashdall—especially as an actor."[16] Clearly, the amateur dramatics which were a key part of Rashdall family life had an impact. It was at Harrow, too, that he developed his love for English literature, for Tennyson, Browning, and

---

hair. He always looked at early School as if he were half asleep—a foretaste no doubt of his gift of concentration. He seemed to me to draw in knowledge through his skin." Bodl. Lib., MS. Eng. misc. c. 590, fol. 92r, Indecipherable correspondent to P. Matheson, 13 December 1926.

[14] Bodl. Lib., MS. Eng. lett. c. 134, fols 112–13, Butler to Rashdall, 9 January 1905.

[15] Matheson, p. 26.

[16] Bodl. Lib., MS. Eng. lett. d. 353, fols 58–9, C. J. Vaughan to Canon Harvey, 15 November 1875. In 1877, as Head of School, Rashdall gave the traditional Latin oration, the *Contio*, at that year's speech day. One imagines he had some headmasterly assistance in its composition.

Dickens in particular, and took the opportunity of the proximity of London to visit museums and galleries, and to indulge his interest in the law by attending court hearings. He was later to write that practising law would have been a serious alternative to ordination for him. A friend reminisced:

> He once told me that, if he had not become a clergyman, he would like to have been a London Police Magistrate, and send to jail, without the option of a fine, the aristocratic rowdies and Under-graduates who make scenes in Piccadilly. He said that they should be punished the same as working men.[17]

It was the breadth and depth of Rashdall's intellectual engagement and curiosity from a young age which Butler identified when writing to his former pupil in 1881, to commiserate with him on the unexpected award of a second-class degree at Oxford:

> I hope the result of the Final Schools was not a great disappointment ... You have a far greater gift for historical, philosophical and theological studies than most able men and you are not formed by nature to show your strength in examination. I shall always think of you as a First Classman in disguise, more likely to write and think originally on the great problems of life than nine tenths of your ablest Oxford contemporaries..

It was from Butler that the religiously precocious Rashdall discovered the attractions of a more liberal theological outlook, which drew him away from the predominant evangelicalism of his family background and upbringing. In particular, it is likely that Butler introduced him to a book to which Rashdall proclaimed his indebtedness until the end of his life, Sir John Seeley's *Ecce Homo*. When *Ecce Homo* was published anonymously in 1865, it caused a sensation, with speculation about its authorship ranging from Newman and Gladstone to George Eliot and,

---

[17] Bodl. Lib., MS. Eng. Misc. c. 590, fol. 83r, Hugh T. Dutton to C. G. Coulton, 17 December 1925.

bizarrely, Napoleon III. The book was an attempt to write a life of Christ as a human being in history, concentrating on his moral teaching and paying little attention to subsequent theological speculation about him. The "young man of promise", to use Seeley's memorable phrase, is seen principally as a moral exemplar rather than the founder of a church.[18] Rashdall commended *Ecce Homo* to his pupils at Oxford as "the best, I might almost say the only good commentary on the New Testament in existence".[19] Towards the end of his life, he commended the book to a correspondent as valuable for its spiritual content, while admitting that "considered as an historical study of the life and teaching of Christ, it is now out of date ... ".[20]

Butler, as a prominent broad churchman, had ample opportunity to draw his protégé's attention to liberal theological thinking such as Seeley's. In the year before Rashdall had arrived at Harrow, Butler and Seeley had both become members of the Church Reform Association, along with Thomas Hughes, the former pupil of Thomas Arnold at Rugby and the author of *Tom Brown's Schooldays*. The aim of the association was the promotion of such Arnoldian reforms as increasing the influence of the laity in the Church of England by establishing church councils in

---

[18] For a detailed discussion of the book and its reception in Victorian England, see Ian Hesketh, "Behold the (Anonymous) Man: J. R. Seeley and the Publishing of 'Ecce Homo'", *Victorian Review* 38:1 (2012), pp. 93–112. The phrase, "young man of promise", appeared in the preface to the original edition, as explained by Sir Oliver Lodge in his introduction to the 1908 edition: Sir John Robert Seeley, *Ecce Homo* (London: J. M. Dent, 1908), p. viii. Seeley was Regius Professor of Modern History at Cambridge, 1869–95, and is best known for his book, *The Expansion of England* (1883), which advocated the idea of "Greater Britain" in his discussion of British imperial history. This concept came under the spotlight in 2022, as part of a campaign to remove Seeley's name from the history faculty library in Cambridge. Another of Butler's Harrow pupils, Charles Gore, was also enthusiastic about *Ecce Homo*.

[19] Matheson, p. 79.

[20] New Coll., PA/RAS/6/2, Rashdall to unknown correspondent ("Dear Madam"), 5 September 1922, quoted in Matheson, p. 216.

every parish, abolishing the need for clergy to subscribe to the Thirty-Nine Articles, and a relaxation of the rules governing church services, some of which were to be concerns of Rashdall later in his career.[21]

Rashdall therefore arrived as an undergraduate at New College, Oxford in 1877 with his mind and character significantly formed by his time at Harrow. He found at New College an environment congenial to their further development and flourishing. Although he left it from time to time, the college was to be the environment which would continue to nurture him as student, teacher, and priest.

The college at which Rashdall arrived with an open scholarship was in the middle of a "remarkable and rapid renaissance".[22] From being a somnolent backwater in 1850, small in number and academically undistinguished, it became one of the three or four pre-eminent colleges in Oxford by the end of the century, aided by two successive university commissions which insisted on new college statutes and ended the historic restriction on fellowships and scholarships to members of Winchester College. Thus reformed, New College flourished and provided an increasingly stimulating intellectual and social environment for its students, of which Rashdall took full advantage.[23]

Rashdall's degree course was Literae Humaniores ("Mods and Greats"), a four-year programme of the study of Latin and Greek language and literature, ancient history, and classical and modern philosophy. It was the standard Oxford humanities course of the day, deemed to provide

---

[21] For the CRA, see A. M. G. Stephenson, *The Rise and Decline of English Modernism* (London: SPCK, 1984), pp. 25-6.

[22] William Hayter, *Spooner: A Biography* (London: W. H. Allen, 1977), p. 38.

[23] New College during Rashdall's time there is described by Alan Ryan, "Transformation, 1850-1914", in John Buxton and Penry Williams (eds), *New College Oxford 1379-1979* (Oxford: The Warden and Fellows of New College, 1979), pp. 72-106. On p. 100, Ryan, one of Rashdall's successors as a philosophy tutor at the college, describes Rashdall as "obviously a benign and effective tutor". Prichard took a different view: "He was not exactly a sympathetic teacher. It did not come natural to him to approach the difficulties of a pupil from the point of view of the pupil. He preferred to present him with the truth as a completed result." Pritchard, art cit., p. 7.

a comprehensive education in the humanities and to establish the habits of critical thinking which would advantage students in whatever walk of life they subsequently followed. At its best, it enabled able students to range widely in their reading and thinking and exposed them to some of the most original minds then at work in their fields. Rashdall took advantage of this, attending, for example, the lectures of T. H. Green, whose idealist philosophy and theology attracted almost a cult following, and benefitting from a joint arrangement between New College and Balliol, one of the first in Oxford, to have tutorials with Benjamin Jowett. Both men had an important influence on him. As did, in a different way, his tutor at New College, W. A. Spooner, known today, if it all, for his Spoonerisms, very few, if any, of which he actually uttered. Spooner and Rashdall had a long association, first as tutor and pupil, later, from 1895, as fellow tutors, and finally, from 1903, when Spooner became Warden of New College. It was a cordial relationship, with the older man keeping a benign eye on his younger, fierier colleague, offering the occasional quiet word of advice to temper Rashdall's enthusiasm. An historian of the college reports a tradition that "Spooner, on being asked if there were any Christian Socialists in New College, replied 'Yes, there are two, Rashdall and myself, but I am not much of a Socialist and Rashdall is not much of a Christian.'"[24]

In the conventional sense, Rashdall was not an outstanding undergraduate, achieving second classes in both Mods and Greats, somewhat to the disappointment of his teachers but owing something, perhaps, to those lapses in exact textual scholarship and his appalling handwriting, which Butler had despaired of at Harrow. He had, however, two significant academic achievements largely unrelated to his degree work, winning the Stanhope Essay prize in 1879 for an essay on Jan Hus, and the Chancellor's Essay prize in 1883, for an essay on the medieval universities, which he was to expand into his first book. He also took full advantage of the other opportunities offered by Oxford, speaking regularly at the Oxford Union during his early years, joining the Oxford University

---

[24] Hayter, *Spooner*, p. 82. At p. 80, discussing Spooner's religious beliefs, Hayter notes his view "that Anglicanism taking it all in all is for Englishmen at any rate the best working hypothesis that has yet been invented".

Rifle Volunteer Corps, and continuing his enthusiastic, if chaotic, efforts at playing sport. Surviving correspondence with contemporaries suggests that they already regarded him as something of a character.[25]

—

Not having gained a sufficiently good degree to make him a strong candidate for a college fellowship, although he sat the examination for at least two, Rashdall decided to take Spooner's advice and stay in Oxford to continue studying, particularly in philosophy and theology. During this time, largely taken up with his work on the history of the universities, he also taught at Oxford High School, a newly founded girls' school, and examined for the cathedral school in Gloucester. Then, in 1883, came the opportunity of moving to a permanent teaching post, which took him away from Oxford for five years, first to St David's College in Lampeter and then, later in the same year, University College, Durham.

It would be easy to characterize the years from 1883 to 1888 as an interlude, yet they had a significant part in Rashdall's development as a scholar and teacher. The teaching load at both Lampeter and Durham was less demanding than an Oxford tutorship and gave him the spare time to continue his historical research on the medieval universities. His membership of two small academic institutions also provided the opportunity for close relationships with colleagues. These included, in Lampeter, T. F. Tout, the distinguished medieval historian, and John Owen, the future Bishop of St Davids, and, in Durham, Archibald Robertson, a church historian and Master of Hatfield College, later Principal of King's College London, before becoming Bishop of Exeter in 1903, and Frank Jevons, a polymath who succeeded Robertson at Hatfield and was later Professor of Philosophy and Vice-Chancellor at Durham. Robertson and Jevons were the dedicatees of *The Universities of Europe in the Middle Ages*. That he looked favourably on this time can be seen by his application for the principalship at Lampeter in 1888, although he

---

[25] The reputation stuck. In the archives at New College there are three undated pen and ink drawings, by G. E. D., of Rashdall as a fictional bird, called the "Rasher-bill" *Divers Oxoniensis.*

confessed to his mother that he was relieved not to be elected, as it kept open the possibility of an eventual return to Oxford.[26]

A significant event during his time in Durham was his ordination, as deacon in 1884 and priest in 1886. The ordaining bishop was J. B. Lightfoot, a biblical scholar and theologian of massive learning, for whom Rashdall had a great regard. Although he did not have a parish post—he was ordained to the chaplaincy of University College—he took his share in conducting services in surrounding parishes, a common practice at the time which was much appreciated by the local clergy. He was to continue this practice throughout his time in Oxford, either through taking services locally or accepting locum positions elsewhere during the vacations.

One of those ordained alongside Rashdall was George Lanchester King, a future Bishop of Madagascar, with whom Rashdall was to keep in touch. King had been one of Lightfoot's "Lambs", the ordination candidates for whom the bishop had a particular responsibility, and was ordained to a curacy at Tudhoe Grange, then a mining village eight miles from Durham. Rashdall would walk out to visit King, reflecting to his wife years later, "King used to say in those old days that my ideas might be all very well in their way, but that they would not do for Tudhoe Grange, and that used to settle it for him!" Occasionally Rashdall would come to preach for King and try out an extempore sermon. After one such effort, a woman in the congregation said that if the young man wanted a call anywhere, he would have to learn to preach better.[27]

In November 1888, Rashdall was able to tell his mother that his wish to return to Oxford had come true and that he had been elected to a fellowship at Hertford College. He wrote to her that he thought

---

[26] Matheson, p. 49.

[27] See *Bishop G. L. King: The Man and his Message* (London: SPCK, 1941). An unpaginated version of this anonymous work is at <http://anglicanhistory.org/england/mbfurse/king1941.html>, accessed 20 July 2023. In his unsuccessful application for the principalship of Lampeter in 1888, Rashdall wrote, "It may, perhaps, be worthwhile to add that, though I have never held a Curacy, I have had a good deal of preaching in neighbouring Churches and a little experience of Parish work." Bodl. Lib., MS. Eng. Misc. a. 16, fol. 52r.

the fellowship was "probably on the old terms—tenable during life or celibacy. Young ladies must therefore be studiously kept out of my way."[28] He was appointed as the philosophy tutor for those reading Greats and also gave university lectures on moral philosophy. It was at Hertford that he met, and became close to, W. R. Inge, then a junior fellow of the college and, later in life, a famous Dean of St Paul's Cathedral. At the time, they had much in common, although they were later to diverge, both theologically and politically, as Inge became more conservative. Inge became noted as the foremost British scholar on the philosophy of Plotinus and was also responsible for introducing the serious study of Christian mysticism, a religious phenomenon for which Rashdall retained an acute scepticism. It was said by Oxford wits of the time that Rashdall did not believe Christianity was true, but wished it was, while Inge knew it was true, but wished it was not.[29]

To Rashdall's duties at Hertford was added, in 1894, the chaplaincy of Balliol College, at the invitation of the Master, Edward Caird. It was an unusual arrangement, designed for one year in the first instance, by which he retained his fellowship and teaching at Hertford, while living in Balliol and taking responsibility for the chapel services. It appears that Caird, an absolute Idealist in philosophy, the revered teacher of William Temple, and a continuer of T. H. Green's tradition of "lay sermons", had hoped to attract Rashdall to a teaching fellowship in theology, in addition to the chaplaincy role, but this was not to be. The somewhat unsatisfactory compromise came to a swift end in 1895, when Rashdall, head-hunted by his old tutor, W. A. Spooner, and H. W. B. Joseph, was offered a fellowship in philosophy at New College, his old college.[30] He accepted with alacrity.

The scene was now set for a more settled existence. Apart from his appointment to a part-time canonry at Hereford Cathedral (where he spent five months a year) in 1910, Rashdall remained at New College until he moved to Carlisle in 1917, living first in rooms in the college

---

[28] New Coll., PA/RAS/4/2, Rashdall to E. M. Rashdall, 20 November 1888, quoted in Matheson, p. 52.
[29] Adam Fox, *Dean Inge* (London: John Murray, 1960), p. 58.
[30] New Coll., PA/RAS/5/2, Rashdall to E. M. Rashdall, 3 March 1895.

and then, after his marriage in 1905, at 18 Longwall Street, a house on the perimeter of the college grounds. For the five years 1899–1904, he was Preacher at Lincoln's Inn, an appointment which provided the opportunity for regular visits to London to mix with the legal establishment and preach a course of sermons, published as *Christus in Ecclesia: Sermons on the Church and its Institutions*, which he regarded as a supplement to *Doctrine and Development*.[31] Apart from holidays in continental Europe—Switzerland was a favourite destination—the only substantial periods he spent away from the workplace were for his study leave in Germany, 1903–4, and a lecture and preaching tour to Canada and the United States in 1913.[32] His loyalty to New College remained intense; to the normal teaching and administrative burden expected of a fellow he added service in such college offices as Dean of Divinity and Sub-Warden. His funeral took place in the college chapel, and he is buried close by in the Holywell Cemetery.

—

Rashdall's return to New College at the age of 37 provides a convenient point at which to break the narrative of his life and take stock. The stage was now set for his work as a popular tutor and lecturer, a respected scholar and author, and an influential preacher and public speaker, much in demand in pulpits and lecture halls. An assessment of his public persona is the subject of the following chapters. It is important, however, to note here a more private aspect of his life, yet one which was inextricably bound up with his public work—his marriage in 1905 to Constance Makins.

As with so much of his personal life, his courtship and marriage were played out in view of his mother and sister. Indeed, Agnes Rashdall appears to have had a crucial role in fostering the relationship, as a friend of the Makins family, near neighbours in London. Rashdall wrote to his mother in August 1903:

---

[31] For the Lincoln's Inn appointment, see Matheson, pp. 90–1, 101, 111.

[32] Details of his North American tour, including a meeting with ex-President Taft, are in Matheson, pp. 142–6.

> I am longing to hear from Aggie whether she has managed to entice Miss M to join her anywhere abroad in September ... If Miss M is to be with her, I should wish to lose no time.[33]

And again, from Switzerland three weeks later:

> On the other hand I am much disappointed to hear that there is almost no chance of Miss M coming to the Lakes. I shall go on with Aggie for the present but must not waste a great deal of time in gadding about unless she after all manages to get round her hard hearted father who pretends to object to their travelling alone, but more probably does not like the expense. I must hope, almost against hope, for another opportunity in that quarter. It was very good of you to facilitate the meeting.[34]

The Rashdall women evidently did not relax their efforts to achieve a successful outcome, for in March 1904 he wrote, this time from Berlin while on sabbatical:

> I was greatly rejoiced at the contents of Aggie's letter. For the rest, I am hopeful. That is all that I can say. It is very good of you and Aggie to do so much for me.[35]

In April the following year, Rashdall was warmly received by the Makins family, on holiday in Minehead, and he and Connie became engaged, getting married on 22 July that year, following negotiations over the marriage settlement. Rashdall was 47, his bride some 15 years younger. She was the eldest daughter of Henry and Kezia Makins. Henry, a wealthy barrister, owed most of that wealth to the shrewd business dealings of his Yorkshire banking family: the marriage settlement involved some tough negotiating. He used much of his wealth to commission new houses in London from the leading architects of the day and to amass a collection

---

[33] New Coll., PA/RAS/5/2, Rashdall to E. M. Rashdall, 23 August 1903.
[34] *Ibid.*, 10 September 1903.
[35] *Ibid.*, 4 March 1904.

of Pre-Raphaelite art—John Everett Millais was a near neighbour—which was to form the nucleus of the pre-eminent private collection of its kind. Rashdall was marrying into a cultured and well-connected family. Although two of Connie's younger brothers were killed in the First World War, her elder brother, Ernest, was a successful soldier and later MP. His son, Roger Makins, later Lord Sherfield, became a significant public figure, not least during his time as ambassador to the United States.

It was a happy and quite conventional marriage. Connie was no wallflower; amongst other things, she was an enthusiastic amateur cellist, organizer of good works, and sprightly hostess and correspondent, addressing her formidable mother-in-law as "Dear Madre". But she was largely content to follow the life then expected of the wife of an Oxford don and, later, a Canon of Hereford and Dean of Carlisle. After Rashdall's death, she returned to Oxford, where she had many friends, for the rest of her long life, living in a substantial house on the Banbury Road and acting as the guardian of Rashdall's memory and keeper of his flame. She made sure that a biography was written, eventually choosing Percy Matheson, a New College colleague, for the task; wrote a letter to the journal *Theology* in defence of her husband's theology in 1935; and donated the remainder of his papers to the Bodleian Library in 1953. She also gave a portrait and some silver to his old college, together with money to fund a studentship in theology. Under the name Constance Hastings Rashdall, she published a play on the life of St Frideswide, the patron saint of Oxford. She died in 1958 and is buried with Rashdall in Holywell Cemetery, under the striking memorial which she commissioned from the sculptor Henry Tyson Smith, a tall Celtic cross made from Westmorland slate and with designs inspired by ancient crosses from the diocese of Carlisle.

2

Dean of Carlisle

In 1917, Rashdall's life took an unexpected turn. In his sixtieth year, he was well established and respected in the world of scholarship and a noted protagonist in debates about church reform and university governance, proposed changes to the divorce law, and other topical issues. His opinions carried weight and were recognized as such even by those who disagreed with him. He was a stirrer and provoker of thought, indefatigable in his search for truth and justice. Moreover, he had a secure base from which to exercise this influence. His tenured post as fellow of an Oxford college, together, latterly, with the opportunities provided by his canonry at Hereford, gave him an independent platform from which to express himself, relatively untrammelled by the institutional pressures and expectations of holding public office or the sheer drudgery of the work involved. When his friend Hensley Henson became, amid a storm of controversy, Bishop of Hereford in 1918, he wrote to Rashdall:

> My life for the past month has been a hideous hustling about the counties of Hereford and Shropshire, taking confirmations, and spending tracts of good time at railway junctions and in the slowest of trains. The waste of time, money, and energy is excessive.[1]

The thought of Rashdall himself becoming a bishop had occurred to some, but it was not to be. He would have made an unlikely, and probably frustrated, bishop. A contemporary said of him that while Rashdall

---

[1] Bodl. Lib., MS. Eng. misc. c. 589, fols 52–3, Henson to Rashdall, 19 March 1918.

reverenced the office of bishop, he despised nearly all the holders of it.[2] That was a little unfair but, as something of an outsider himself in ecclesiastical circles, and as a doughty supporter of other outsiders, he perhaps lacked something of the empathy or institutional intelligence to hold together a disparate group of people or views. Personal charm counted for much in his dealings with people but his lack of sympathy for, or imaginative grasp of, other points of view could be abrasive. He would have found the advice given to Mandell Creighton when he moved from a Cambridge professorship to be Bishop of Peterborough in 1891—that he would no longer be required to teach, but to edify—hard to accept. To be fair to Rashdall, he was sufficiently self-aware to recognize that he would be ill suited for episcopal office. Writing to a friend, he said:

> But I personally have not the slightest desire for such a position. I do not have the qualifications for it, I am too old to begin it, and it would prevent my doing the particular things which I want to do i.e. to express myself freely in books and otherwise.[3]

In any event, Rashdall did not rely on the vagaries of episcopal patronage to further his career. He tried the more conventional academic route, as a candidate for the Waynflete Chair of Moral and Metaphysical Philosophy at Oxford in 1910, the year of his election as a Fellow of the British Academy, and was subsequently considered for further Oxford professorships in philosophy and theology. His biographer, who was a close colleague at New College, suggests that the wide range of Rashdall's published work, covering a number of disciplines and subjects within disciplines, was too eclectic for those responsible for such appointments, who preferred candidates with a deeper and narrower knowledge of their particular field.[4] Rashdall himself, writing to his Hereford colleague

---

[2] Bodl. Lib., MS. Eng. Misc. c. 590, fol. 82r, Hugh T. Dutton to C. G. Coulton, 17 December 1925.

[3] Rashdall to the Revd W. J. Ferrar, 15 June 1917, quoted in Matheson, p. 178.

[4] Matheson, pp. 127–8. Prichard wrote, "It was indeed a source of wonder that he managed to cover so much ground. The explanation, however, is probably to be found in his somewhat matter-of-fact temperament, which

A. L. Lilley in February 1910, expressed his desire to succeed to the Regius Professorship of Divinity, vacated by the death of William Ince, but doubted whether any government would be bold enough to offer it to him.[5]

Those outside the enclosed worlds of academic and ecclesiastical politics, however, saw in Rashdall someone capable of making an important contribution to national life. In 1912, the Prime Minister, H. H. Asquith, suggested Rashdall's appointment as Dean of Durham. The only two people he thought had the necessary qualifications were Rashdall and Hensley Henson, with Rashdall, in Asquith's view, being the better qualified: "He is the only clergyman in the Church who, as far as I know, has real claims to philosophic distinction", he wrote to the Archbishop of Canterbury, Randall Davidson, although his views "might be too much of a shock for such an atmosphere". After further consultation with the archbishop, Henson was appointed.[6] Five years later, in May 1917, Asquith's successor, David Lloyd George, manifested his own fondness for mavericks by appointing Rashdall as Dean of Carlisle. The Rashdalls were faced with packing up two homes, in Oxford and Hereford, in time to move north for his installation in July.

Writing to a friend who congratulated him on his appointment, Rashdall took a tongue-in-cheek view of the opportunity awaiting him:

> A Bishop writing to congratulate me said that he regarded it as the function of a Dean to do and say things which a Bishop could not do or say without upsetting the apple-cart. I intend to endeavour to perform that function, but I do not aim at being sensational—not even so much as my brother of Dunelm [Henson].[7]

---

enabled him to make up his mind rapidly and to be satisfied with solutions which to others might savour of the nature of short cuts." H. A. P[richard]., "Dr. Hastings Rashdall", *Hertford College Magazine* 13 (April 1924), p. 7.

[5] St Andrews University Library, Lilley Papers, MS. 30705, Rashdall to Lilley, 14 February 1910.

[6] Bernard Palmer, *High & Mitred: Prime Ministers as Bishop-Makers 1837–1977* (London: SPCK, 1992), p. 166.

[7] Matheson, p. 178, Rashdall to the Revd W. J. Ferrar, 15 June 1917.

Although not as prestigious a deanery as Durham, the move to Carlisle provided a contrast to life in Oxford and Hereford. Carlisle and its immediate vicinity had a population of just under 80,000 at the time, with probably some 60,000 living in the growing city itself. By contrast with the surrounding rural areas, the city was an industrial centre. Although the textile industry was declining, engineering and food manufacture were thriving and Carlisle was a thriving railway centre, an important junction in its own right with what was to become the largest marshalling yard in Europe on the edge of the city. Railway lines ran behind the wall of the deanery garden and the noise of the trains was a constant interruption. When Rashdall's predecessor complained to the railway authorities about the noise of the shunting, it is said that engine drivers made sure to add an extra whistle, "for the dean". To the activity and social problems of any early-twentieth-century industrial city, especially in poverty, housing, and education, the outbreak of war brought additional challenges. There were two large munitions factories close at hand, the East Cumberland National Shell Factory in the city itself and a big depot at Gretna to the north. A number of buildings in the city were requisitioned as military hospitals. Drunkenness, particularly among munitions workers, became such a problem that the government took over public houses and breweries in 1916, in order to restrict licensing hours and reduce alcohol consumption.

Carlisle thus provided Rashdall with the opportunity to pursue his interests in a more focussed way and to earth them in a local context. To this task, he addressed himself with characteristic enthusiasm, and he soon became an acknowledged and respected figure in city life, and its principal representative in church matters. He had the advantage of geography in this respect. The largely rural diocese of Carlisle covered the counties of Cumberland and Westmorland together with the detached part of Lancashire where Barrow-in-Furness, another of the few industrial outcrops, was situated. The city and cathedral of Carlisle were at the northern tip of this large area and the bishop lived some five miles from the city, at Rose Castle. Deans of Carlisle had, therefore, a considerable degree of freedom of operation within the city. Rashdall was particularly fortunate in having cordial working relationships with the two bishops in his time: John Diggle, a fervent patriot and popular preacher who had come from significant ministries in industrial Liverpool and Birmingham, and, after Diggle's death in 1920, the contrasting figure of H. H. Williams, whom Rashdall had known in Oxford, where Williams was first a philosophy tutor at Hertford College and then Principal of St Edmund Hall.[8] In addition, the suffragan bishop of Barrow-in-Furness, Campbell West-Watson, was a residentiary canon at the cathedral until he moved closer to Barrow in 1921—he and Rashdall got on well, and West-Watson's young family were welcome guests at the deanery. The other residentiary canons were welcoming and supportive, among them the long-serving John Eustace Prescott, who had been appointed a canon in 1870, becoming archdeacon of Carlisle in 1883 and later chancellor of the diocese, dying in harness in 1920, and H. D. Rawnsley, at the end of a remarkable life which had included the co-founding of the National Trust.[9]

The presence of able and congenial colleagues, whom Rashdall could trust, meant that he was able to devote time and attention to other matters than the administration of the cathedral. Not that he was at all negligent. He preached regularly—although a number of his hearers, despite their awareness of being in the presence of a powerful mind, found it difficult to follow his train of thought—oversaw changes to the pattern of services, and was always keen to place the cathedral at the centre of local life, particularly with the events surrounding the Armistice in 1918 and the subsequent post-war commemorations. But he was often away from home, either in London or elsewhere in the country, attending meetings, giving talks and lectures, and playing his part in the war effort through

---

[8] Rashdall wrote to Mrs Humphrey Ward, the novelist, "His theological opinions are so moderate that I hardly know what they are. Probably he is mildly and not unorthodoxly liberal." New Coll., PAR 6/1, Rashdall to Mrs Humphrey Ward, Carlisle, 30 December 1919.

[9] Prescott's successor, both as archdeacon and chancellor, Ernest Campbell, contributed information about Rashdall's time as dean to Matheson's biography, see *op. cit.*, pp. 231–4.

his involvement with that branch of Naval Intelligence preparing for the eventual peace negotiations. His national profile remained prominent.[10]

What his position in Carlisle enabled him to do was to relate these broader concerns to local interests. The scope of his engagement was impressive. As well as the ecclesiastical meetings and committees one would expect, Rashdall's name featured constantly in the local newspapers.[11] He chaired the local branch of the League of Nations Union, the largest and most influential organization in the British peace movement of the time, and gave speeches, not uncritical of the League, about its importance in any post-war settlement. He spoke on divorce law reform, of which he was a cautious advocate, on poor law reform, and about the poor housing and sanitary conditions in the city, which won him the approval of local Labour politicians. A forum for these discussions which he particularly enjoyed was the revival of the pre-war Carlisle Parliament, of which he became Speaker, with the mayor as his deputy. He was impressed by the insight and the breadth of knowledge of the local representatives.

Nor did he neglect his educational interests. Some of this came with the job. As dean, he was *ex officio* chair of governors at Carlisle Grammar School, carefully steering the school through financial challenges and an at times sensitive relationship with the city council. He spoke at numerous speech days and prize-givings at schools throughout the diocese and beyond. He was instrumental in reviving the local branch of the Historical Association, as well as the Christian Social Union. But he went beyond the call of duty in his support of the Workers' Educational Association, acting as a tutor as well as a committee member. He wrote to his Oxford friend Webb on the last day of the war:

---

[10] Rashdall's pass as a member of the Admiralty War Staff, Intelligence Division (No. 83, dated 13 April 1917) survives in the Bodleian Library at MS. Eng. misc. a. 16, fol. 245.

[11] See Dorothy Postle and Margaret Marsh, *Hastings Rashdall, Dean of Carlisle 1917-1924* (Whitley Bay: Dorothy Postle, 2000), for an exhaustive summary of Rashdall's time as dean, as evidenced in newspaper reports.

> I am taking a class for the WEA in Ethics. Among the people who attend is an elderly man who is a self-taught philosopher and reads Hegel![12]

No account of Rashdall's time in Carlisle would be complete without special mention of his ecumenical sympathies, cultivated during his academic career but carried over into his public ministry in Hereford and Carlisle. His policy as dean was always to give the Free Churches a place in the cathedral's worship on major public occasions, for example the Peace Thanksgiving service in July 1919. This was at a time when even to have a nonconformist minister reading a lesson in the cathedral was the cause of comment. Outside the cathedral building he could do more, whether at open air services or at meetings of clergy. The Revd H. H. Summers, Congregationalist minister in Carlisle at the time, recalled Rashdall's impact:

> From his first coming to Carlisle he showed a friendliness which won a real response from the nonconformists of the city... In a very short time he brought the clergy of the Church of England and the ministers of the nonconformist Churches into closer and more cordial relationship. He instituted a bi-monthly conference, "The Fraternal", where we might meet in friendly intercourse and discuss the problems which we saw from different angles. These meetings were held at Dr Rashdall's invitation in the Deanery and were attended by some twenty of us—ten Anglicans and ten Nonconformists. Among the subjects discussed were Religion and Natural Law, Education, Church Government, Orders and Sacraments. I cannot say that we were able to find solutions that were satisfactory to everybody, but I am quite sure that we understood each other better and respected each other more after

---

[12] New Coll., PA/RAS 6/1, Rashdall to C. C. J. Webb, 11 November 1918. There is a syllabus, list of students, and lecture notes for his class on political philosophy at Bodl. Lib., MSS. Eng. Misc. a. 16, fols 158–78.

those talks. There was there an atmosphere of friendliness and high seriousness. For this we were largely indebted to the Dean.[13]

It was the relationship of trust engendered by such meetings that led the members of the Carlisle Free Church Ministers' Fraternal to send Rashdall a letter of support after the Girton Conference in 1921:

> From your various important writings, Sir, and your part in not a few local conferences on matters theological and practical we have learned to regard you with peculiar pride and affection, as one of the most learned, fearless, and convinced defenders of the central realities of that great and blessed Christian Gospel which we hold in common and do our little best to proclaim.[14]

Rashdall replied:

> ... no manifestation of sympathy which I have received publicly or privately has afforded me so much pleasure and consolation as the letter which you sent me signed by every Free Church minister in Carlisle.[15]

This correspondence may stand as a tribute to the seriousness of Rashdall's ecumenical vision and his determination to relate the truths of the Christian faith to the world around him.

Amid all the activity there were shadows. Rashdall's health, which had caused concern since before he came to Carlisle, took a distinct downturn in 1922. During that year, he had four operations, for hernias and bowel cancer, and his remaining years were marked by medical treatment and the subsequent periods of convalescence.[16] His wife was convinced that the stress caused by the intense criticism which followed the Girton

---

[13] Matheson, p. 235.
[14] Ibid., pp. 208–9.
[15] Ibid., p. 209.
[16] New Coll., PA/RAS, 6/2, Rashdall to P. F. Rowland, The Deanery, Carlisle, 14 August 1922.

Conference had contributed significantly to his poor health.[17] A sign of his own awareness of the likely outcome was his refusal of the invitation to give the prestigious Gifford Lectures for 1922–4, which held out the prospect of another major contribution to philosophical and theological scholarship and might have stimulated him to follow his work on the atonement with an exploration of the doctrine of the incarnation. The death of his mother in May 1923 brought to an end a long and close relationship, perhaps the most important in his life. As in all things, he showed great courage and determination, struggling to fulfil speaking and preaching engagements and going to Switzerland with Connie in August for their last holiday together. After another operation in late December, he was taken to Worthing to convalesce. He never recovered and died there on 9 February 1924, at the age of 65. His funeral took place in New College Chapel on 13 February, with a simultaneous memorial service in Carlisle Cathedral. He was buried in Holywell Cemetery, a few hundred yards from the college which had been so much a part of his life.

It would be easy to think of Rashdall's six and a half years in Carlisle as an unusual postscript to a largely academic career. He did not write a major work while he was there—he didn't have the time to do so—his energy was spread thinly over a wide range, and his final years were beset by ill health. Yet his time as dean enabled him to engage his sympathies in new ways, allowed different sorts of people to get to know him, and earthed him in a context which brought out the best in him. Carlisle undoubtedly took notice of him and honoured his memory. The cathedral bells, refurbished and augmented in his memory by his widow, still ring on his birthday; until 2009 the Dean Rashdall Memorial Fund offered scholarships to young local people studying at Oxford; and there is a street in the city—Rashdall Road—named after him.

---

[17] "But so soon as peace was signed my husband's succession of illnesses followed partly caused by his persecution which he felt severely & which culminated in his two year fight with cancer ...", Bodl. Lib., MS. Eng. Misc. c. 590, fol. 6r, Constance Rashdall to J. N. L. Myres, 31 March 1953.

3

Rashdall the historian

Those who only know Rashdall's work from the study of their own discipline are often surprised by the range of his expertise. Historians are unaware that he was a major philosopher and theologian; theologians are blissfully ignorant of his stature as a moral philosopher; philosophers do not realize that his work on the medieval universities has more than stood the test of time. It was a remarkable achievement for one person to produce major contributions to three disciplines, not to mention the plethora of articles, sermons, reviews, and letters which flowed from his pen, as well as his active involvement in church affairs.

There are two preliminary comments worth making. The first is that Rashdall was first and foremost a teacher. Apart from *Universities of Europe in the Middle Ages* and *The Theory of Good and Evil* (although the latter included previously published material), all his significant published work had its origins in lectures and sermons. The second comment, which perhaps follows from the first, is that there is an inconsistency about Rashdall's thought—rough edges, loose threads, the occasional blind spot—which makes difficult, and ultimately unrewarding and misleading, the task of creating a systematic account of it.

There are, nonetheless, principles and themes which are consistent in his life and thought. The first of these, and the key to making sense of some of the others, is his interest in history and, more particularly, the development and interplay of ideas in differing historical contexts. This marks his approach not only to his conventional historical work but also, for example, to his use of scholastic philosophy and theology, and his approach to New Testament criticism. How people thought about the truth and how they used that thinking to lead their lives was of enormous interest to him and provides a connecting thread to much of his work.

His historical prowess was recognized by others. His colleague, H. W. B. Joseph, wrote of him:

> He had a real historical gift, and was especially interested in the movements of thought, and loved to trace the leaven of new ideas at work in past and present. Indeed, his power was probably greater in this direction than in pure speculation, notwithstanding his love of argument and his great interest in philosophical issues.[1]

That historical awareness was present from an early age. Schoolboy letters, articles in the school magazine, and a diary of 1874, when he was 16, show evidence, within his general intellectual curiosity, of a particular interest in historical characters and their impact. Commenting on his reading of *Napoleon's Table Talk*, he wrote:

> At all events, [it] makes me believe Napoleon was human, which I was inclined to doubt before. And unless he was a monstrous hypocrite in every word he said, there must have been a good deal that was good in him. I believe he was a sort of fanatic, very much like Oliver Cromwell.[2]

Five years after that diary entry Rashdall displayed clear evidence that he possessed significant gifts as an historian. His winning 1879 Stanhope Historical Essay prize entry at Oxford, *John Huss*, was published. Many years later an undergraduate contemporary wrote to Rashdall's widow, enclosing his copy of the essay, and commenting: "I am amazed that a young man of 21 could have produced a work showing such learning and such wisdom."[3]

John Huss shows the precocious scholar announcing themes which were to become consistent in his thinking—an interest in medieval

---

[1] Matheson, p. 250.

[2] Bodl. Lib., MS. Eng. Misc. e. 361, fols 55v–56r.

[3] New Coll., PA/RAS, 7/3, Edward? Cook to Constance Rashdall, 17 September 1932.

philosophy and theology, the importance of universities for progressive thinking, an admiration for those who, like Hus and Wycliffe (he was later to write the article on Wycliffe for the *Dictionary of National Biography*), stand up for the truth against the crippling constraints of institutional authority. In Hus's case, this authority was represented by the Council of Constance, at which he was sentenced to be burnt at the stake in 1415, thus creating a martyr both for the cause of the reform of the Church and for Bohemian nationalism. Rashdall wrote of Hus:

> The great work of John Huss was to make a protest on behalf of the rights of Conscience ... This conscientiousness, this scrupulous sincerity, was the source of all his Protestantism.[4]

And he concluded the essay:

> There was in him nothing of the braggadocio of the Puritan: nothing, on the other hand, of the ostentatious humility of the Medieval Saint. Few men who have enjoyed so much popularity, and that the dangerous popularity of the religious leader, have been so absolutely free from affectation. His life was devoted to the assertion of a great principle which had been abused for centuries. No man was ever less of a demagogue, no man was ever more gentle or more humble; yet it may be doubted whether a whole people ever conceived such an enthusiastic affection for one who was so worthy of it.[5]

If one university prize had ignited Rashdall's interest in medieval intellectual history, another enabled him to lay the groundwork for his greatest contribution in this field. His decision to spend two years in Oxford after completing his degree, reading in philosophy and theology, gave him the time and space to reflect more deeply on medieval history and scholastic theology, as a result of which he entered for and won the Chancellor's Essay prize in 1883, writing on the medieval universities.

---

[4] *JH*, p. 38.
[5] *JH*, p. 41.

Unlike his essay on Hus, this one was not published, but it provided the foundation for *Universities of Europe in the Middle Ages*. That he was able to produce such a remarkable work owed something to the fact, which has already been noted, that his first two teaching posts, teaching classics at Lampeter and Durham, did not make the demands on him which would have been the case with an Oxford tutorship, and put him in close contact with colleagues who were able to nurture and stimulate his work. Tout in particular provided early encouragement, securing from Rashdall an article on "The Universities of Oxford and Cambridge" for Volume 1 of Cassell's *Illustrated History of England* (1886).

In the preface to *Universities*, Rashdall reflected ruefully:

> I entered upon it with no intention of undertaking anything more than such a revision and expansion of my Essay as would justify its publication in book form. The Essay was, of course, written in less than a year: the revision has occupied more than eleven. Twelve years will seem none too much to any one acquainted with the extent and difficulties of the subject: but it is fair to myself to state that I have been throughout pretty fully occupied in teaching subjects quite unconnected with medieval history.[6]

Looking back on Rashdall's life, one of his Oxford pupils, P. F. Rowland, remarked:

> Rashdall used to deplore that his book on that subject had taken up so much of his life; but his love of thoroughness made him read any new book that came out that shed light on his theme, and the publication was repeatedly deferred on that account.[7]

The obsession did not abate. Towards the end of his life, he was snatching time in the British Museum in order to make preparations for a new edition. This had to wait until after Rashdall's death. The revised edition, edited by F. M. Powicke and A. B. Emden, was published in 1936 and is

---

[6] *Universities*, I, p. v.
[7] New Coll., MS. PA/RAS, 6/2.

still regarded as the standard work on the subject, the "revised Rashdall" appearing frequently in texts and citations.[8]

What has made *The Universities of Europe in the Middle Ages* such an enduring success? In the first place, Rashdall drew on an unusually extensive range of primary sources, both published and unpublished, travelling to France and Spain to consult them. His biographer records Tout's comment, meeting Rashdall at the Bibliothèque nationale in Paris, that the "slight sketch" of Rashdall's original essay was now becoming "a serious and permanent contribution to historical literature".[9] Immersion in the sources was a stimulus to creative thinking. Secondly, the depth of engagement with the sources is complemented by the breadth of the subject matter. Rashdall explained that "the plan of this book is to describe with tolerable fulness the three great archetypical Universities,—Bologna, Paris, Oxford,—and to give short notices of the foundation, constitution, and history of the others, arranged in national groups." This he certainly achieved, covering the whole of Europe, which is what makes the book an invaluable work of reference to this day. But he went beyond that. The chapter on "Abelard and the Renaissance of the Twelfth Century" set the intellectual context for the development of the universities as centres of teaching and debate, while providing themes which were to recur in his later work as a philosopher and theologian. The long chapter on "Student Life in the Middle Ages" has fascinating material ranging from meals and discipline to academical dress and "the wilder side of University life", with evidence ranging from the tariffs for the punishment of various kinds of assault (with fines increasing the closer one got to actually hitting the person who was the target of your stone) to the prohibition of chess, described by the Visitor of one Oxford college as "noxious, inordinate, and unhonest".[10] Rashdall was keen to point to some continuities with his own experience of university life when it came to "sconcing", the practice

---

[8] Larry Siedentop, for example, claims that the 1936 edition "can hardly be bettered" on the emergence of the universities in Europe. Larry Siedentop, *Inventing the Individual: The Origins of Western Liberalism* (London: Allen Lane, 2014), p. 383.

[9] Matheson, p. 42.

[10] *Universities*, II, pp. 614, 671.

of requiring students, or their seniors, to drink a quantity of wine or beer in one go as punishment for a breach of college etiquette or discipline. At the Sorbonne in the fifteenth century, for example:

> A Doctor of Divinity is sconced a quart of wine for picking a pear off a tree in the College garden, or again for forgetting to shut the Chapel door, or for taking his meals in the kitchen. Clerks are sconced a pint for "very inordinately knocking" at the door during dinner, 2s. for being very drunk and committing "many insolences" when in that condition, or a pint for "confabulating" in the court late at night, and refusing to go to their chambers when ordered, or for asking for wine at the Buttery in the name of a Master and consuming it themselves.[11]

Finally, in the opening chapter and the epilogue, are Rashdall's reflections on the nature of a university, which make interesting reading in the light of twenty-first-century debates about the purpose of higher education. At the very end of the book, Rashdall summarizes what he believes are the essential qualities of a university. There are two of them. The first, he says, "is to make possible the life of study, whether for a few years or during a career". The second is, "to bring together ... face to face in living intercourse, teacher and teacher, teacher and student, student and student".[12]

The life of study and personal contact—a community of learning. Have these two things, Rashdall says, and everything else is window-dressing. Faculties, examinations, degrees, vice-chancellors, professors, sports clubs are all no doubt valuable, but they are secondary, they are not the object of the exercise and are only useful if they contribute towards it. But without these two things a university loses its animating principle. "It would be a fatal error", Rashdall writes, "to imagine that either the multiplication of books or the increased facilities of communication can ever remove the need of institutions which permit of such personal

---

[11] Ibid., pp. 618–19.

[12] Ibid., p. 714.

intercourse."[13] That was written in 1895—it would be interesting to know how Rashdall would react to online and distance learning; and to our modern means of communication.

Why the stress on personal interaction? Because, says Rashdall, "there is a kind of knowledge which can only be secured by personal intercommunication, a kind of intellectual cultivation which is only made possible by the constant interchange of ideas with other minds, a kind of enthusiasm which is impossible in isolation."[14] And that is entirely appropriate for the essence, the identity, the soul of a university. The word "university", like its Latin root *universitas*, means merely a number, a plurality, an aggregate of people.[15] It is the interaction of people in a community of learning that is essential for a university. Get that wrong and a university will lose its soul.

The three volumes of *The Universities of Europe in the Middle Ages* are not only a work of deep historical scholarship, although it is the scholarship which has enabled them to endure and was recognized by Oxford in the award of the Doctor of Letters degree (DLitt), much to the wry amusement of his sister: "I have made myself a DLitt. I don't know why: Aggie will say 'Vanity.'"[16] They were also for Rashdall a kind of manifesto, a statement of concerns which were to occupy him for the rest of his life—the search for truth, not as an abstract and detached entity but as an active component in human flourishing; the place of institutions, particularly universities and the Church, in providing a structure for that search to continue; and the potential for the great scholastic theologians, from Abelard to Aquinas, to be a resource for modern thinking and living.

The importance of institutions as the embodiment of a society's ideal was stated right at the beginning of the book:

> The University, no less than the Roman Church and the feudal hierarchy headed by the Roman Emperor, represents an attempt to realize in concrete form an ideal of life in one of its aspects.

---

[13] *Ibid.*

[14] *Ibid.*, p. 715.

[15] *Ibid.*, I, p. 7.

[16] New Coll., PA/RAS, 5/2, Rashdall to E. M. Rashdall, 19 October 1901.

> Ideals pass into great historic forces by embodying themselves in institutions. The power of embodying its ideals in institutions was the peculiar genius of the medieval mind, as its most conspicuous defect lay in the corresponding tendency to materialize them. The institutions which the Middle Age has bequeathed to us are of greater and more imperishable value even than its Cathedrals.[17]

Rashdall's interest in the history of educational institutions was not wholly exhausted by *Universities*. He had contributed articles on New College and Hertford College to Andrew Clark's *The Colleges of Oxford* (1891) and published, with R. S. Rait, a comprehensive history of his own college, *New College*, in 1901.[18] He had originally undertaken this latter work on his own but, in a way typical of him, he had bitten off more than he could chew, so Rait was drafted in to complete the project.

Rashdall's historical work was not, however, simply another string to his bow, an interesting sideline to be pursued in his spare time. On the contrary, it was integral to his project and provided him with a model to be transposed into the present day. The intellectual revolution of 1150 to 1250 presented him with an agenda which he saw as acutely relevant to the needs of the modern Church, not to be slavishly copied, which would be absurdly anachronistic, but with clear clues about the priorities which needed to be addressed. These included a rational approach to theology from a firm philosophical basis, the reinvigorating of the Church's ministry, and the reform of institutions, such as universities and theological colleges, to equip people to address the challenges of their time. At one point he suggested the possibility of writing a modern version of Abelard's famous treatise, *Sic et non*:

> If I had the time and the learning, I should like to write a new "Sic et Non" with a view of showing how vain is this pretence that the Church has always taught one and the same thing—that there is a fixed, compact, definite body of doctrine, one stereotyped

---

[17] *Universities*, I, p. 5.
[18] Hastings Rashdall and Robert S. Rait, *New College* (London: F. E. Robinson & Co., 1901).

interpretation of doctrine, which has been thought and taught always, everywhere, by all.[19]

Speaking in 1899, four years after the publication of *Universities*, Rashdall used the example of Thomas Aquinas as a resource for contemporary theological thinking:

> Thomas Aquinas did a great work for his time by putting Christianity into a shape in which it satisfied, on the whole, the intellect of his day—by combining the truth about God which the world had learned from Christ with all the truth about man and the Universe which it had learned from other sources—and chiefly from ancient Greece. But knowledge and thought go on growing, and the work which St Thomas did for *his* age wants doing again for ours; for knowledge increases and thought advances, and Theology, if it is to be a living science, must advance too. The greatest idea that we owe to St Thomas is his magnificent conception of Theology as a science in which the results of all other sciences, the highest generalizations in all departments of thought, are summed up and harmoniously combined in a great theory about the ultimate meaning of the world—about the relations between God, the World, and Man. That ideal is one which we want to keep steadily before our eyes, for it is an ideal still more valuable than any positive doctrine which is to be found in his writings.[20]

In a later talk on "The Scholastic Theology", Rashdall reinforced this point:

---

[19] Bodl. Lib., R. H. 110, No. 13, fol. 2, lecture on "The Obligation of the Creeds", undated but with office stamp, 30 September 190?. It is headed in MS "For Church Congress", but none of the Church Congress addresses mentioned by Matheson fit the description.

[20] "St Thomas Aquinas", *God and Man*, p. 198.

> In the first place the Schoolmen ordinarily show a magnificent faith in Reason which is not always exhibited by modern theologians, and which is absolutely abhorrent to a large proportion of modern religious people. They believe that God gave us Reason to be used, not (as appears to be thought in some quarters) for the express purpose of deceiving us. These men really grappled with the intellectual difficulties of their age. The great danger to the faith in those days was the newly discovered Aristotle, the Averroism of the Arabic philosophers and their European disciples, and the materialism into which their Averroism tended to degenerate in the minds of the physicians and other crude sceptics of the age. They really grappled with these difficulties and constructed a system of the Universe which satisfied the highest intellects of Europe for some three centuries and longer. Our difficulties are different. To us Darwinism, the higher criticism, historical discovery, are what Aristotle and Averroes were to the men of the Thirteenth Century. If Christianity is to retain its hold upon the thinking and cultivated portion of the world, these difficulties must be grappled with in the spirit, though not by the method, of St Thomas Aquinas.[21]

That he did not see this enterprise as the preserve just of professional theologians is illustrated by his intriguing conclusion to the talk on Aquinas:

> And yet it is not always through the work of professional theologians that the new Christian thought of our age—the Christianization of the new knowledge and the intellectual reconstruction of the old faith—reaches the majority of educated men. Much of the best theology of our age, for instance, is to be found in Poetry. But it would be absurd to say that Tennyson and Browning have done for their age exactly the work which St Thomas did for his...

---

[21] "The Scholastic Theology", *Ideas and Ideals*, p. 172.

And yet it is probable that many will find and have found in the poetry of Tennyson and Browning what they have been unable to find in the writings of the Theologian and the sermons of the Preacher. The study of St Thomas is now confined almost entirely to the priest and the professional student, but the ideas of St Thomas still live for the untheological world of culture in the poetry of Dante.

Even so it is perhaps through the expression it has found in the poetry of Tennyson and Browning that the professed theological teaching of the age that is just passing away will contribute most to that fuller, richer, completer understanding of the Christian faith which is the heritage—let us not doubt it—of ourselves and for our children.[22]

---

[22] *God and Man*, pp. 201–2. Rashdall was typical of his generation in his admiration for Tennyson and Browning, particularly Browning, and how they might contribute to the contemporary articulation of Christian faith. He particularly commended Browning's long poem, "Christmas-Eve and Easter-Day" (1850), to his students, with its stress on individual integrity in the face of competing religious claims. (Matheson, p. 79.) William Temple was another Browning devotee, and W. R. Inge wrote on both poets. Browning's wider appeal to philosophers is evidenced, for instance, by the Cambridge personal Idealist McTaggart. John McTaggart Ellis McTaggart (1866–1925) makes a number of appearances in this book. A Fellow of Trinity College, Cambridge, where he spent the whole of his working life, McTaggart was a dominant figure in the Cambridge philosophy of his day until his Idealist thinking was challenged by a younger generation, particularly his former pupils, G. E. Moore and Bertrand Russell. The bulk of his work is now largely unread, although his argument that time is unreal still attracts attention from philosophers. He was an unusual figure: a convinced atheist from an early age, who was a supporter of the establishment of the Church of England, largely for political reasons, he believed in reincarnation and thought that ultimate reality was best described as a community of spirits united by love. His great work, *The Nature of Existence* (1921–7), explains this system, along with a defence of his teaching on the unreality of time. His smaller popular work, *Some Dogmas of Religion* (1906), attracted wide interest, particularly

While Aquinas, Abelard, and the scholastic theologians more generally provide Rashdall with intellectual resources for the challenges which he thinks the modern Church faces, he is stimulated as well by the energy and focus brought by the new religious orders of the time, the Dominicans and Franciscans, which replaced a sophisticated and settled monastic culture with a more radical and disruptive approach to mission, evangelism, and social concern. In his chapter on the University of Paris in Volume I of *Universities*, he devotes 50 pages to "The Mendicants and the University", tracing the shift of higher education away from the old monastic orders to the secular clergy, the arrival on the scene of the new orders of friars founded by Dominic and Francis of Assisi, and their rapid impact on university life and the teaching of theology:

> Just at this crisis in the intellectual history of Europe, two great minds, S. Francis and S. Dominic, conceived almost independently and simultaneously a wholly new ideal of monastic perfection. The educational and social usefulness of the older Orders had been, it may be said, almost accidental... To the Friars Preachers [Dominicans] and the Friars Minors (*sic*) [Franciscans] on the other hand was assigned not a wilderness to be turned by patient labour into a retreat in which some foretaste of the repose and the worship of Heaven might be enjoyed by souls weary of earth, but a world to be Christianized. To the Mendicants the calm, monotonous round of solemn service was but a subordinate object: the end of their existence was the salvation of souls. Like the great modern order [Rashdall means the Jesuits] which, when their methods had in their turn become antiquated, succeeded to their influence by a still further departure from the old Monastic

---

at the time of the First World War, when its arguments for reincarnation brought comfort to the bereaved. He and Rashdall had a cordial regard for each other, reviewing each other's work with respect, while acknowledging their divergent views. Rashdall asked McTaggart to read a draft of his *The Theory of Good and Evil*, and received extensive comments in reply.

routine, the Mendicant Orders early perceived the necessity of getting a hold upon the centres of education.[23]

Without going to the lengths of advocating the founding of new religious orders, Rashdall was convinced of the need for the reinvigoration of clergy training and the reform of the ancient universities, if clergy and others were to be equipped as the "missionaries of knowledge" which the Church so urgently needed if it was to bring about a plausible intellectual engagement with contemporary society. If *The Universities of Europe in the Middle Ages* is hardly a manifesto for ecclesiastical reform in the twentieth century, it contains the seeds of the concerns which were to occupy Rashdall for the rest of his working life.

---

[23] *Universities*, I, pp. 346–7.

4

Rashdall the philosopher

If Rashdall's interest in intellectual history was a connecting thread in the development of his thinking, so was his philosophical outlook. At a time when much theology seems to have drifted away from its philosophical moorings, it is easy to forget how closely connected the two disciplines were a hundred years ago. A secure metaphysical foundation was seen as essential to any theological programme which was more than a subjective reliance on religious feeling and experience. The stress on metaphysics gave the philosophy of the time a number of common characteristics. The first was a sense of optimism, of buoyancy of spirit, of confidence in human rationality and its ability to shape circumstances, of an expanding civilization which felt good about itself. The second, related to this, was a belief in the development and evolution of thought—this was, after all, the period when the implications of the evolutionary model, exemplified by Darwin, were being explored in a number of different disciplines. The third was an interest in substance, memorably described by John Macquarrie as "solid enduring thinghood".[1] Whether that substance be material or spiritual, whether there be one or many substances, this somewhat static conceptual model may be contrasted with modern interests in more dynamic concepts such as events, processes, and life. Finally, the philosophy of the period was comprehensive and systematic. The conviction that the universe, and life within it, was rational and explicable led writers to attempt theories of everything. Their ambition may be seen in some of the titles of their books, from Bradley's *Appearance and Reality* to McTaggart's *The Nature of Existence*, to Rashdall's own *The*

---

[1] John Macquarrie, *Twentieth-Century Religious Thought* (London: SCM Press, revised edition 1971), p. 21.

Theory of Good and Evil. Philosophers were intellectually ambitious and thought that they had the nature of reality in their grasp, in a way which would be unusual today.

Within this broad framework, there were many different philosophies competing for attention—materialism, positivism, idealism, for example—as well as differences of approach within each of those categories. Rashdall was a philosophical Idealist. Idealism can be described as a philosophical outlook which privileges mind over matter. The unifying principle in the universe is mind or consciousness—matter does not exist independently of mind. It is a philosophical outlook as old as Plato and includes, in their different ways, thinkers such as Berkeley and Kant. But Rashdall was part of the remarkable flowering of British idealism, or, better, Anglo-American idealism, lasting from about 1860 until the end of the First World War, which issued a stark challenge to any optimistic world view. British idealism grew out of a combination of the philosophy of Plato and Aristotle with that of Kant, but from the very start these ideas were developed in different ways. Some adhered closely to an absolutist Hegelian line, and critics of idealism were not slow to point out that the obscurity of Hegel's thought allowed considerable latitude for ingenious interpretation. Others, like Rashdall himself, were more individualist and Berkeleyan.[2]

Rashdall was critical of Hegel, referring at one point to the "heartless deity of the Hegelians",[3] and he gained more from the work of later

---

[2] For a detailed history of British idealism, see W. J. Mander, *British Idealism: A History* (Oxford: Oxford University Press, 2011); David Boucher and Andrew Vincent, *British Idealism: A Guide for the Perplexed* (London and New York: Continuum, 2012), is a clear introduction to the main themes and philosophers in the movement.

[3] Unfortunately, I have been unable to trace the original source of this quotation. Elsewhere, however, Rashdall refers to "the vague and indecisive kind of Theism which we find in Hegel (if indeed Hegel is rightly understood as a Theist at all". Bodl. Lib., R. H. MSS., Box 105 (R. H. 105), no. 19, lecture on "Kant and after Kant", fol. 19. See also H. A. P[richard]., "Dr. Hastings Rashdall", *Hertford College Magazine* 13 (April 1924), p. 7, for Rashdall's antipathy to Hegel.

German philosophers, such as Lotze and Pfleiderer, who were important conduits of the Hegelian tradition to the English-speaking world.[4] Hegel, like many of his contemporaries, believed that reality is rational, and that the world is a manifestation of a spiritual principle. His was, therefore, a form of absolute idealism, the belief that physical objects and our finite human minds are related to an all-embracing experience, the absolute, in which they are somehow absorbed. It was this approach which found expression in the work of British absolute Idealists, such as Bradley and Bosanquet.

Rashdall, on the other hand, was a personal Idealist. From 1898, he was one of a group of Oxford philosophers who met regularly to develop the notion of personal Idealism as a distinct strand of Idealist philosophy. He contributed an essay, "Personality: Human and Divine" to the group's collective statement, *Personal Idealism*, edited by Henry Sturt in 1902. Sturt's combative preface to the volume stated that it was intended to counter the twin perils of naturalism—which denigrated the spiritual—from outside the Idealist camp, and absolutism—which gave insufficient recognition to the independence of the individual—from within. For Rashdall, personal Idealism meant a stress on the individual mind or spirit, as an entity that was created but was not part of some universal or absolute consciousness, as the absolute Idealists believed. Self-consciousness is our best window into the nature of God. In 1898, he had written:

---

[4] Rudolf Herrmann Lotze (1817–81) was a major philosophical figure at the end of the nineteenth century. The teacher of Ritschl and widely read on both sides of the Atlantic, he was regarded as being of similar importance to Kant and Hegel in the history of German philosophy. He had a medical degree and made significant contributions to the study of psychology as well as philosophy: his bringing together of scientific and philosophical thought aroused great interest and he became, like Bergson a little later, very fashionable for a time. Rashdall called him "The great and truly Christian thinker, Lotze" and engaged with his thought in *The Theory of Good and Evil*. Bodl. Lib., R. H. MSS., 106, 1, undated MS. sermon on "The Problem of Evil".

> What I do want to insist upon is the irrationality and inconsistency of first pretending to interpret the Universe in terms of mind, and then substituting for mind as we know it a one-sided abstraction of pure thought which is unlike anything that we know or have any reason to believe to be possible. The whole tendency of modern speculation confirms the natural tendency of the religious consciousness to interpret the Universe in terms of Mind. So far the Christian thinker will welcome its results; only let us have the courage to say that, if we accept so much, we will not be juggled into accepting some miserable abstraction in place of the living God by that old bugbear of philosophical polemics, the charge of anthropomorphism. Of course our God is anthropomorphic: and so must be every God whom the mind of man can really conceive.[5]

In his 1902 essay, he went on to make the connection between God and the human personality:

> Just the same line of thought which infers that God knows perfectly the world which we know imperfectly points to the belief that He possesses perfectly the personality which we possess imperfectly—that He is a being who thinks, who persists throughout his successive experiences, who knows those past experiences as well as the present, who distinguishes Himself from the objects of his thought, who in particular distinguishes Himself from all other consciousnesses, and, finally, who wills, and wills in accordance with the conception of an ideal end or good.[6]

---

[5] *Doctrine and Development*, p. 277.

[6] Henry Sturt (ed.), *Personal Idealism: Philosophical Essays by Eight Members of the University of Oxford* (London: Macmillan, 1902), p. 376. For a comment on Rashdall's contribution to the volume, stressing his atypical approach in some respects, see Mander, *British Idealism*, p. 367. For an engaging modern account of the attraction of personal idealism in theological thinking, see Keith Ward, *Personal Idealism* (London: Darton, Longman & Todd, 2021).

"Who in particular distinguishes Himself from all other consciousnesses ..." Because, for Rashdall, the human personality is impervious, a finite consciousness which cannot be assimilated or absorbed into a greater consciousness, he has to accept that God is not infinite, nor is he omnipotent, in the terms of the traditional definition of God as omnipotent, omniscient, and wholly good. The Absolute, insofar as that term has meaning for Rashdall, is not God, but God and the aggregation of finite consciousnesses or minds: "The Absolute, therefore, if we must have a phrase which might well be dispensed with, consists of God and the souls, including, of course, all that God and those souls know and experience."[7]

There were two further consequences for Rashdall's thinking in this respect. The first is that he was dismissive of the phenomenon of mysticism; he simply could not comprehend what mysticism could mean or how it could work, if it was impossible to think of the individual soul as being somehow lost in some greater whole. In this, he was at odds with his old friend, W. R. Inge, who almost singlehandedly reacquainted the Church of England with the treasures of the English mystical tradition. Nor, secondly, was he much persuaded by arguments from religious experience. Writing to C. C. J. Webb in 1920, he explained:

> I don't believe in a "specific" religious emotion: the religious emotions (which vary very much) seem to me to be made up of emotions which we do feel towards other objects, ie chiefly towards persons.

Baron von Hügel, also writing to Webb, was one of a number to comment on what they saw as a striking blind spot in Rashdall's outlook:

> I dare say that, had I known him when I was quite young and if he had been my senior, I should have felt only his ethical greatness and not his—surely—strangely great lack of the specifically religious sense—or, at the very least, of the mystical element of religion. He has established himself permanently in my mind as

---

[7] Ward, *Personal Idealism*, p. 392.

a living example of how greatly ethical a soul can be with little of the specifically religious sense.[8]

Although Rashdall's interest in moral philosophy and ethics pervades much of his writing, it reached its fullest expression in his second major work, *The Theory of Good and Evil: A Treatise in Moral Philosophy*, published in two volumes in 1907, and the result of some 20 years' thought. The dedication page gives a clear indication of what he was trying to achieve: "To the memory of my teachers Thomas Hill Green and Henry Sidgwick." Green, philosopher and lay theologian, himself influenced by Hegel, was one of the most influential of the early British Idealists. Although intellectual doubts held him back from ordination, his *Introduction* to the collected works of Hume, the *Prolegomena to Ethics*, and the *Lay Sermons* attracted a wide readership, and he was known for his promotion of social action in the city of Oxford. He had an extraordinary impact on a generation of Oxford students, including Rashdall, Henry Scott Holland, and Charles Gore, becoming a guru for many of them, and the shock of his early death in 1882, the year after Rashdall graduated, served only to enhance his reputation. This was reinforced by his appearance as a main character in Mrs Humphrey Ward's bestselling novel of Victorian faith and doubt, *Robert Elsmere*, in 1888. Sidgwick, for many years professor of moral philosophy in Cambridge, had a longer-lasting influence on the development of British philosophy. His great work, *The Methods of Ethics*, first published in 1874 and continually revised by him until his death in 1900, attempted to respond positively to the utilitarianism of J. S. Mill by reconciling it with the best of the earlier British philosophical tradition of "moral sense" or intuitionism. In recent years, there has been a revival of interest among

---

[8] Michael de la Bedoyere, *The Life of Baron von Hügel* (London: Dent, 1951), p. 311 n. 1.

moral philosophers in Sidgwick's work, which is seen as a significant resource for the discussion of current ethical issues.[9]

In *The Theory of Good and Evil*, Rashdall attempted to bring together the idealism of Green with the sophisticated and developed utilitarianism of Sidgwick into what he called "ideal utilitarianism". For Rashdall, the morality of an action, rule, policy, or institution is not determined simply by a hedonistic calculation—"the greatest happiness of the greatest number"—but by the value or goodness of the state of affairs it results in, the greatest amount of good upon the whole. The value of a state of affairs is determined, therefore, not only by the sum total of pleasure it produces but by the sum total of the goods of virtue, knowledge, and pleasure. And, moreover, virtue, knowledge, and pleasure in that order—there is, for Rashdall, a hierarchy of goods. Moral behaviour is judged by the value of life as a whole rather than how things are going at a particular point in time.

That "ideal utilitarianism" is an ambitious undertaking was recognized at the time and some early critics were sceptical about whether Rashdall had succeeded. The anonymous reviewer in *The Times* explained that, in this balancing act:

> Dr Rashdall stands nearer to Sidgwick than to Green in his formal attitude of mind and his method of approaching the ethical question. At the same time the actual conclusions (technicalities apart) are much nearer those of Green than might appear from the inappropriate and inadequate chapter devoted to Green's formula in the Second Book.[10]

---

[9] For Sidgwick's vigorous afterlife in the philosophical literature see, for example, Roger Crisp, *The Cosmos of Duty: Henry Sidgwick's "Methods of Ethics"* (Oxford: Clarendon Press, 2015); Derek Parfit, *On What Matters* (Oxford: Oxford University Press, 2011), Volume One, *passim.*, but particularly pp. xxxiii–xl, 130–49. At p. xxxiii, Parfit describes Sidgwick's "great, drab book *The Methods of Ethics . . .* " as " . . . I believe, the best book on ethics ever written."

[10] *The Times*, 26 September 1907.

The reviewer in *The Athenaeum* was even more dismissive, claiming that, "Mr Rashdall describes his theory as Ideal Utilitarianism, but this epithet by itself conveys no meaning whatever, as, indeed, he shrewdly suspects", and concluding that Rashdall's ethical theory is "... in essence very simple, and does not take us very far".[11]

On the other hand, there was a recognition that the work provided a stimulating introduction to moral philosophy. It drew appreciative reviews, as well as letters of gratitude. The book sold well, and Rashdall provided corrections for a second edition, which appeared after his death, in 1924. A balanced contemporary judgement was offered in 1928 by C. C. J. Webb, a close friend and colleague of Rashdall (and indeed his best man) but by no means an uncritical follower:

> Nowhere is the centrality in Rashdall's thought of his personal conviction of the absolute reality of the individual personal consciousness more clearly seen than in his ethics, his "theory of good and evil". He was a moralist to the core, and his book bearing that title, although in importance as a contribution to the branch of learning concerned it is probably to be ranked below either of his other two principal works, should long hold its own as an introduction to its subject. No English treatise known to me can be preferred to it in this respect as covering the ground and giving to the student a sense of being engaged with real issues, theoretical and practical. We find Rashdall's point of departure, here as elsewhere, that of the idealistic reaction ... against the empiricism and hedonism which had in the heyday of Mill's influence dominated the philosophy of this country. But, here as elsewhere, he could not advance .. in the direction of subordinating the importance of individual personality either to an impersonal moral law or to a social organism with a "good" of its own distinct from the "good" of the individual persons composing it. He preferred to define his own position as "Ideal Utilitarianism", agreeing with the older Utilitarianism in finding the criterion of right action in its conduciveness to a good which

---

[11] *The Athenaeum* 4182 (21 December 1907), p. 790.

could be realized in a personal consciousness, but differing from it in refusing to regard pleasure as more than one among several elements in that "good".[12]

Webb also noted that, somewhat surprisingly given his insistence on the importance of the individual human consciousness, Rashdall was a determinist and was opposed to what he termed "indeterminism" in other writers. Webb writes: "It must be borne in mind that he was only enabled to reconcile this determinism with his denial that the evil present in human wills and actions had its source in God by his refusal to regard God as in the strict sense of the word omnipotent."[13]

Rashdall himself summarized his position at the end of the chapter on "Free Will" in *The Theory of Good and Evil*:

> Determinism of the kind I have suggested has nothing in it paralysing or depressing to the most strenuous moral effort. To my own mind it is far more inspiring than most Indeterminist theories of the Universe. It represents God as the ultimate source of all being in the Universe that has a beginning, and as directing the world-process towards the goal which shall attain as much of the highest ideally conceivable good as can become actual. He calls upon the higher spiritual beings who have derived their existence from Him to aid in this process. It is a real, and not a merely apparent, struggle to which their God-derived moral consciousness invites them. The evil is a real evil, though an evil destined to be more and more diminished. The rapidity with which and the extent to which the evil will be diminished and the good attained really does depend in part upon human effort. It is

---

[12] Matheson, p. 242. Clement Charles Julian Webb (1865–1954) was a significant lay theologian and moral philosopher of the time. A Fellow of Magdalen College, Oxford, he also taught philosophy at New College (before Rashdall's return as a Fellow) before being elected in 1920 as the first Nolloth Professor of the Philosophy of the Christian Religion until his retirement in 1930. Webb was the brother-in-law of Rashdall's colleague, H. W. B. Joseph.

[13] Matheson, p. 244.

true doubtless that God knows how much each of us is capable of aiding towards the process, and how much he will aid; but we do not know, and no human being can ever know until he has acted. And there is nothing in these considerations to paralyse, but everything to quicken and reinforce, all those desires and aspirations which determine the extent and manner in which we shall actually be permitted to take part in the great process of world-redemption.[14]

The struggle of good against evil is not, for Rashdall, simply a striking title for a book, but a serious existential engagement.

—

By the time *The Theory of Good and Evil* was published, it was becoming clear that the philosophical tide was beginning to turn against the Idealism which had been so dominant, in Oxford at least, and towards realism; a journey which was to lead to the analytical and linguistic philosophy for which Oxford became famous later in the century. There was a similar movement in Cambridge, with philosophers such as Bertrand Russell and G. E. Moore reacting against the Hegelianism of McTaggart and others.[15] In a lecture on "Idealism", probably written shortly before the First World War, Rashdall himself recognized the decisive move:

> It is a matter of common knowledge among those who take any interest in philosophical speculation that the dominant tone of English philosophy during the last half-century has been idealistic: and that the centre from which proceeded the wave of idealistic thought is Oxford ... In less than a decade all this has been changed. If any body was to ask what system was predominant in Oxford at the present moment, I am afraid he would have to say "Realism". The question of the source of

[14] *TGE*, II, pp. 354–5.
[15] Moore had published his famous essay, "A Refutation of Idealism", as early as 1903.

this Realism is almost too personal a one for public discussion. I believe the ultimate source of it is to be found in the teaching of Professor Cook Wilson.[16]

Rashdall's younger Oxford colleague, R. G. Collingwood, who was elected to a fellowship at Pembroke College in 1912, found himself thrust into a philosophical and political battleground, in which the surviving Idealists, whom Collingwood categorizes as "the school of T H Green", were assailed by the Realists, marshalled by John Cook Wilson, who had become Wykeham Professor of Logic in 1889 and thus a Fellow of New College, where he was therefore a colleague of Rashdall's. In his *Autobiography*, Collingwood wrote:

> The game was thus left in the hands of their opponents [i.e., the opponents of the school of Green]. These called themselves "realists", and undertook the task of discrediting the entire work of Green's school, which they described comprehensively as "idealism"... When I say that Green's school at this time obsessed Oxford philosophy, what I mean is that the work of the school presented itself to most Oxford philosophers as something which had to be destroyed, and in destroying which they would be discharging their first duty to their subject. The question what positive views they themselves held was of secondary importance. The leader of this school was John Cook Wilson, the professor of logic. He was a fiery, pugnacious little man with a passion for controversy and an instinctive eye for its tactics ...[17]

---

[16] Bodl. Lib., R. H. MSS., 106, no. 7, fols 1 and 4. Although undated, internal evidence suggests that it was written while Rashdall was in residence in Hereford, i.e., between 1910 and 1917. In 1920, Rashdall acknowledged to Webb that his own views had been modified during this period: "My opinions have been modified, since we knew each other, quite as much as yours ... after all my Idealism has been a good deal modified." New Coll., Rashdall papers, PA/RAS 6/2, Rashdall to Webb, Carlisle, 13 March 1920.

[17] David Boucher and Teresa Smith (eds), *R. G. Collingwood: "An Autobiography" and Other Writings: With essays on Collingwood's life and work* (Oxford:

There can be no doubt that Cook Wilson and his followers have had the greater prominence in the subsequent philosophical literature, with Rashdall and his fellow Idealists slipping quietly out of view, for such is the pattern of intellectual development. Such modern interest as there has been in Rashdall's moral philosophy has seen him more as an interesting historical figure in the development of Idealist ethics than as a compelling ethical teacher like Sidgwick. Anthony Skelton, for example, has provided a careful comparison of Rashdall's approach with that of another ideal utilitarian, G. E. Moore, whose *Principia Ethica* was published in 1904. Rashdall comes out well from the comparison: "Rashdall therefore seems to make a more lasting and perhaps more significant contribution to the defence of ideal utilitarianism than does Moore" and "Rashdall did open up a new avenue for the defence of ideal utilitarianism, which makes the study of his works important to understanding the development and the philosophical viability of this position."[18] Yet Skelton also notes the essential instability of Rashdall's position and is critical of some of his arguments. "His position is therefore an unstable middle view between uniformly monistic classical utilitarianism on the one hand and uniformly pluralistic deontological intuitionism on the other."[19]

Oxford University Press, 2013), pp. 18–19. This edition reprints *An Autobiography* as first published in 1939, together with some minor writings, and a series of biographical and interpretative commentaries by Collingwood scholars. For the Oxford philosophical background, see James Patrick, "The Oxford Man", pp. 213–45, and Michael Beaney, "Collingwood's Critique of Oxbridge Realism", pp. 247–69. It is worth noting that one of Cook Wilson's principal lieutenants on the realist side was Rashdall's fellow philosophy tutor at New College, H. W. B. Joseph. Matheson recalls the amusement of their colleagues at the vigorous and long-running philosophical debate between Rashdall and Joseph, Matheson, p. 82.

[18] Anthony Skelton, "Ideal Utilitarianism: Rashdall and Moore", in Thomas Hurka (ed.), *Underivative Duty: British Moral Philosophers from Sidgwick to Ewing* (Oxford: Oxford University Press, 2011), pp. 45–65, quotation at p. 65.

[19] *Ibid.*, pp. 52–3; see also Mander, *British Idealism*, especially pp. 367, 404–5.

Rashdall's interest in casuistry, the attempt to apply general moral principles to specific cases, has also attracted some contemporary interest, given the rapid growth in areas, particularly medical ones, where ethical considerations become a formal part of the decision-making process. His main contribution to this subject is his 1894 article, "The Limits of Casuistry", much of which was reused in the chapter on casuistry in *The Theory of Good and Evil*. Rashdall asks whether the moral philosopher should be regarded as an expert who can give a definitive answer to complex ethical questions and concludes that the appropriate role for such a person is to provide a framework to enable the relevant agent to come to an answer for themselves:

> I may put what I have been saying in another form by saying that the function of the moral philosopher in the decision of ethical questions is rather that of the judge than that of the jury. Consulted as to what a man ought to do under such and such circumstances, he will not, *qua* moral philosopher, say, "You should do this or that," but rather he will explain the relevant principles of the Moral Law, apply them to the facts of the case, and then say, "If you think that this action will produce such and such results, then do so and so; if not, don't" ... Such is the way the moral philosopher will sum up the case, whether to his own conscience or to somebody else. The moral philosopher is the judge, the conscience and judgment of the individual (whether the philosopher himself or his client) are the jury.[20]

Commenting on Rashdall's position, the contemporary philosopher, Sarah McGrath, commends his wisdom and prescience:

> ... I believe that something like this model—on which the proper role of the moral philosopher is not to definitively answer the

---

[20] Hastings Rashdall, "The Limits of Casuistry", *International Journal of Ethics* 4:4 (July 1894), pp. 475–6; this passage is repeated in *TGE*, II, p. 442. The original article was read as a paper to the Cambridge Ethical Society in November 1893, with Henry Sidgwick in the chair.

pressing moral questions of "his client," but rather to put the client in a better position to answer those questions correctly on the basis of his or her own judgment—is a popular one among contemporary moral philosophers. The fact that this conception of the proper role of the moral philosopher is also vigorously contested—both by those who think that the moral philosopher should do more, and by those who think that she should do less—is only to be expected, and further speaks to the continuing relevance of the issues raised by Rashdall's essay.[21]

Some of the practical implications of the struggle for good against evil will be discussed in a later chapter on Rashdall's role as a public theologian.[22] In the meantime, what have we learned about his philosophical outlook? We have seen that he was an Idealist, believing the universe to be rational and to have spiritual meaning. For him, the key to unlocking that meaning is the human personality—so he was a personal Idealist. Human self-consciousness is, by analogy, our window into what God is like. As we are thinking, feeling, and acting beings, so is God. "What God is, that man was eternally meant to be."[23] Furthermore, the human personality is finite and impervious; it is not absorbable into some greater whole, whether that be a mysterious Absolute, or some form of social organism. Human freedom, human history, and contingency are important. The struggle against evil is a real one, in which human beings are required to take an active part. They can make a difference and are not simply the passive observers or beneficiaries of God's activity. We have seen also that this stress on personality and personal freedom means that God, for Rashdall, is limited, in the sense that he is finite and not, strictly speaking, omnipotent.

These are, roughly speaking, the main outlines of Rashdall's philosophical position, and they were held pretty consistently throughout his life. They are stated in a way which does not do justice to the

---

[21] Sarah McGrath, "On Hastings Rashdall's 'The Limits of Casuistry'", *Ethics* 125:1 (October 2014), pp. 196–9 (quotation from p. 199).

[22] See below, Chapter 6.

[23] *D and D*, p. 111.

complexity of his thought. Critics at the time doubted whether he had achieved a successful balancing act between personalism and divine transcendence, between idealism and utilitarianism, particularly as there were idiosyncrasies in his outlook; his acceptance of determinism; his dismissal of mysticism. Yet, ultimately, Rashdall thought that he had bigger battles to fight than establishing the clear coherence and stability of a neat philosophical system which satisfied the mind but impoverished the soul. Preaching a university sermon in Cambridge just before Christmas 1889, he said, "I hope it will not be thought a paradox if I say that it was no part of our Lord's mission on earth to teach Theology. He came to teach Religion. I am not one of those who think that you can have Religion without God, or even Religion without Theology. But we must remember that Theology is a Science—a Science whose function it is to set the eternal truths of Religion in their proper relation to all other truths."[24]

Note: The Question of Rashdall's Racism

Rashdall has recently been accused of racism. It is clear, even to the casual reader of his work, that it betrays some of the common prejudices of his time and milieu, including the casual, unthinking racism which was endemic in the British society of his day. It is true, though regrettable, that countless similar examples can be found in the writing of his contemporaries, creating an ugly legacy to which we are now becoming more sensitized. The recent attacks on Rashdall, however, go beyond infelicitous phrasing and unfortunate examples, and claim that racism is intrinsic to his thought. Writing independently of each other, Jeremy Waldron and Gary Dorrien connect the moral philosophy articulated in *The Theory of Good and Evil*, focussing on certain passages in that book, with a racist outlook. Waldron, in his 2015 Gifford Lectures, accuses Rashdall of "deep philosophical racism", while Dorrien asserts that

---

[24] *Ibid.*, pp. 50–1.

Rashdall's defence of ideal utilitarianism "built up to the obliteration of inferior races", and that he was, intellectually at least, a white supremacist.[25]

These are serious charges, which require discussion at a greater length than is possible in a book which is intended as a brief introductory study of Rashdall's thought, without swamping the whole book and changing its direction of travel. Among the issues raised are the need to examine the plausibility of the assertion that the evidence of racist attitudes in Rashdall's work somehow infects and invalidates his whole philosophy, creating, as it were, a geological fault line through it. This would in its turn require a broader investigation of attitudes to race at the time. The problem of attempting to disentangle what is of enduring value in the work of historical figures from ideas which are now regarded as lamentable occurs quite frequently: one thinks, for example, of discussions about Aristotle, Hume, and Kant, some of whose views are now judged to be racist or sexist. Another, more general question is how we assess the behaviour and thought of past figures in the light of their historical context and the conceptual framework within which they operated. Ideas or attitudes which are "normal" or "obvious" at the time can create strong social, psychological, and intellectual constraints to conform with them. What seems obvious to one generation or milieu might be appalling to its successors or in another context. How, to quote the philosopher Amia Srinivasan, do we "draw a distinction between what historical persons might be blamed for, given their circumstances, and what historical actions we ought to condemn, given ours"?[26]

---

[25] Jeremy Waldron, *One Another's Equals: The Basis of Human Equality* (Cambridge, MA: Belknap/Harvard University Press, 2017), p. 20; Gary Dorrien, *Kantian Reason and Hegelian Spirit: The Idealistic Logic of Modern Theology* (Malden, MA and Oxford: Wiley-Blackwell, 2012), p. 401. See also Dorrien's more focussed critique of Rashdall, which repeats much of the same material in "Hastings Rashdall: Post-Kantian Idealism, and Anglican Liberal Theology", *Anglican and Episcopal History* 82:3 (September 2013), pp. 289–317; particularly the section "Liberal Idealism as White Supremacist Utilitarianism", pp. 303–9.

[26] Amia Srinivasan, "Under Rhodes", *London Review of Books* 38:7 (31 March 2016).

That such matters are not discussed further here is in no sense to downplay their importance or to come to a premature judgement about their resolution. It is simply to recognize that their complexity requires a depth of treatment which is beyond the bounds of this book.

5

Rashdall the theologian

However sophisticated a theologian's system might become in later life, there will often be earlier, simpler influences and dispositions which contribute to the finished product. We have already seen how the son of a serious-minded and reflective clergyman, who died when Rashdall was 11, and a dominant mother from a well-connected evangelical family had from very early days a strong moral seriousness and conscientiousness, combined with a fascination for church order and worship. He was to move away from the thoughtful evangelicalism of his parents and his sister, Agnes, but the seriousness of purpose never left him. The search for the truth mattered to him—it was not an intellectual game.

This seriousness was reinforced, and its terms of reference broadened, by encounters in his formative years as a schoolboy and undergraduate. Of these, two are particularly worth noting. The first, as we have seen, was with his headmaster, and housemaster, at Harrow, H. M. Butler, whose liberal churchmanship and broad political sympathies formed a significant influence on Rashdall's own thinking. Then, a few years later in Oxford, he went for tutorials with Benjamin Jowett, the famous classical scholar and theological controversialist, who was by this time Master of Balliol College, where he had served as a tutor for many years. Jowett had the distinction of being vilified by both the evangelical and catholic parties in the Church of England during the intense theological debates of the mid-nineteenth century. It has been suggested by A. O. Dyson that the seeds for Rashdall's liberal theory of the atonement were planted by Jowett.[1] Whether or not that was the case, Rashdall

---

[1] A. O. Dyson, Introduction to Margaret Marsh, *Hastings Rashdall— Bibliography of the Published Writings* (Leysters: Modern Churchpeople's

was certainly indebted both to Jowett's example as a standard-bearer for liberal critical thinking and for his theological outlook. He used to regale his pupils with stories about Jowett and wrote to his mother in 1897: "He was probably the greatest and most successful (I mean in the highest sense) member of our despised and unappreciated profession."[2]

It was to Montagu Butler, "my earliest theological teacher", however, that Rashdall dedicated *Doctrine and Development*, the collection of university sermons which he published in 1898. Although a collection of sermons might sound unpromising territory to the modern mind, sermons of this period were often a vehicle for serious theology. There is probably no better introduction to the scope and style of Rashdall's theological interests than this book, and it is not surprising that he received many letters of appreciation from clergy and laypeople after its publication. The sixteen pieces are more like lectures than sermons, although they retain some of the freshness and rhetorical power of the spoken word. The preface to the work sets the scene and enables Rashdall to announce his intention:

> This volume is intended as a modest attempt to translate into the language of modern thought some of the leading doctrines and ideas of traditional Christianity ... The book may perhaps be found to differ from some of the more familiar English works of the same type by a franker admission of the necessity for theological construction, while I have endeavoured to avoid the opposite mistake of supposing that Religion is possible for reflecting minds without a Theology, or that "liberal" Theology means vague and indefinite Theology.[3]

He goes on:

Union, 1993), p. 3. For Jowett, see Peter Hinchliff, *Benjamin Jowett and the Christian Religion* (Oxford: Clarendon Press, 1987).

[2] Matheson, p. 86.

[3] *D and D*, p. xvii.

> The title (chosen only for want of a better) is intended to suggest two things—that all Theology is the result of development, and that the development of religious thought is not finished yet. Theology arises out of the attempt to set the facts of the moral and religious consciousness in their due relation to the facts of science and of history. It is the attempt to build up a theory of the universe from the religious point of view.[4]

Furthermore, Rashdall's view of doctrinal development implies progress, as a critical age addresses theological statements made in uncritical times:

> Because the Christian thought of the future must be different in many ways from the thought of the past, it need not be less Christian. The Christian thought of the future should be more Christian than the thought of the past, just because we are getting to understand better than past generations the essential and eternal value of that life and that teaching on which all Christian doctrine is a commentary.[5]

Finally, he underlines the strong link between theology and philosophy:

> It is my strong conviction that a Theology which is to satisfy thoughtful men in these days must rest upon the basis of a thorough-going metaphysic; and therefore I do not apologize for becoming a little metaphysical.[6]

Two of the sermons in the volume serve as outlines for themes which Rashdall was to explore at greater depth. "Personality in God and Man" prefigures the essay on "Personality: Human and Divine" in Sturt's *Personal Idealism*, while "The Abelardian Doctrine of the Atonement" is a forerunner of *The Idea of the Atonement in Christian Theology*. The others range widely, from discussions of the doctrine of the Trinity and

---

[4] *D and D*, pp. vii–viii.
[5] *D and D*, pp. xi–xii.
[6] *D and D*, p. xii.

the historical value of the Gospels, to the Christian understanding of property and the different vocations to which Christians are called.

One of the most characteristic of the sermons is that on "Christ and Culture", a university sermon preached in Oxford in 1897. Typical Rashdall themes are brought together. There is the stress on the moral basis of Christianity, rather than the purely dogmatic or intellectual:

> The truths that (Jesus) came to reveal were intensely practical moral and religious truths, not truths of Philosophy, or Science, or Criticism. It is the character of God, his moral relation to us and our relation to Him, not the laws of His government in the Physical Universe, that we see reflected in the life and consciousness of Jesus Christ. The purpose too of His work was all primarily moral—to change men's hearts and wills, not to instruct their intellects. His method again was primarily moral, not intellectual. He appealed to the conscience rather than to the speculative intellect: He moved men by personal influence rather than by intellectual cross-examination. And lastly He founded a Church, whose terms of communion are primarily moral—attachment to a Person and to an Ideal—not a school whose unity depends upon intellectual agreement.[7]

It is on this basis that Rashdall goes on to investigate the nature of the Christian calling in terms of the imitation of Christ:

> One of the difficulties which we encounter in attempting to make the life of Christ a model for our own imitation is the great difference between the actual occupations of His life and what many of us feel are, must be, ought to be, the occupations of ours.[8]

It is easy enough to recognize Christ-like service in the work of clergy and missionaries, the medical profession, philanthropy, even in the work of charitable organizations, schools, and local government. But what

---

[7] *D and D*, pp. 232–3.

[8] *D and D*, pp. 234–5.

of the life of the mind? Where does that fit in? For, "It is more difficult to see how the intellectual life can be Christ-like."[9] Rashdall finds an answer in the idea of sacrifice, the subject of another of the sermons. "True intellectual life, like true practical life, must, in a sense, find itself by losing itself in the life of others." Moreover,

> Intellectual goods must be consecrated, like other good things, by being shared with others—in one way or another—by teaching, by professional work, by public service or the like. The primitive idea of sacrifice, we may remind ourselves, is not self-annihilation, but communion.[10]

At this point, Rashdall draws on his interest in medieval theology to suggest an example:

> I do not know that we sufficiently appreciate the great service which the Mendicant Friars have rendered to the Church by their consecration of the student's life. When we think of a Friar and a Friar's work, we naturally think first of toilsome preaching-journeys and sick-bed ministries, of spiritual counsel and sympathy for the sick and poor. But this was not the only side of the Friars' work. It was mainly to the Friars that Europe owes the absorption of Aristotle into the thought of Christendom. It was the Friars who appreciated, as men had never appreciated before, how a life of love might be spent in diffusing knowledge—secular knowledge no less than religious knowledge—of which humanity had sore need.[11]

Moreover, there is an urgent need now for this ministry:

---

[9] D and D, p. 235.
[10] D and D, p. 236.
[11] D and D, p. 237; see also the references to the mendicant friars in *Universities*, as noted above, pp. 44–5.

> Never in the history of the world has it been truer that the people perish for lack of knowledge. Never has it been more necessary that those who possess knowledge should become, if I may say so, missionaries of knowledge. There is indeed a social value in all knowledge. One of the best things we can do for other people, whether for individuals or for classes, is to help them to love and to enjoy the knowledge and culture which we enjoy ourselves, even without direct reference to any more practical social end.[12]

This need is particularly urgent in two areas—in political, social, and economic thought, on the one hand, and religion, on the other. Rashdall identifies the immense task of theological reconstruction required if the Church is to engage effectively with the culture in which it is set; a task which is just as pressing in our own time as it was then, if not more so.

> There is a demand for a great reconstruction of Christian Theology, such a reconstruction of Christian Theology in the light of our improved knowledge of the Universe as Thomas Aquinas accomplished for his own day at the great crisis when the recovered works of Aristotle represented the world's richest intellectual inheritance. The mere handful of men who are seriously engaged in that great task want many helpers, and still more they want missionaries of the knowledge which they are building up. When we turn from the cultivated few to the great mass—let us say even of ordinary fairly educated people, what a chaos there is in religious belief and no-belief! Everywhere we find religious belief losing its hold on the minds of men on account of the silence of the instructed clergy, the flimsiness of the religious ideas which are taught by the less instructed, and the vagueness and indefiniteness of the only substitutes which are offered in their place by those who have parted company, or all but parted company, with the Christian tradition ... We go on teaching children things which we do not believe ourselves.[13]

---

[12] D and D, p. 239.

[13] D and D, pp. 240–1.

It was a theme to which Rashdall devoted much of his life as a theological educator and to which he was to return, using very similar language, a quarter of a century later in his 1921 sermon.

—

The principal contribution to Rashdall's task of theological reconstruction is *The Idea of Atonement in Christian Theology*. The book had its origins in the Bampton Lectures for 1915 at Oxford but was only published, with the addition of extensive notes and appendices, in 1919, due in part to the exigencies of wartime Britain and in part to Rashdall's move to the deanery of Carlisle in 1917, which restricted the time available to revise the work. Rashdall on the atonement has come to be acclaimed, and sometimes vilified, as a classic statement of the subjective view of the atonement, the understanding that Christ's death on the cross is such an expression of God's love that it inspires us to follow Christ in a life of sacrificial love for others. Christ's action is exemplary. This view is opposed to so-called objective, or penal substitutionary, theories of the atonement, which see Christ's death as a punishment, a ransom, for human sin, which Christ freely accepts on behalf of, and as a substitute for, the human race.

Writing in 1919, Rashdall set out what he had tried to achieve in the lectures:

> One of the most crying needs of the Church at the present moment is a serious attempt at re-thinking its traditional Theology. A large part of that theology has obviously become more or less unintelligible to modern men who do not possess technical knowledge of its history and contents. It needs to be re-examined, and (where necessary) reconstructed, in the light of modern philosophy, modern science, and modern criticism. How far the ancient formulae should be frankly abandoned, or how far they admit of re-interpretation in terms of modern thought and experience, is a question on which for the present there are likely to be considerable differences of opinion ... Personally, I am heartily in favour of the more conservative course of

preserving (as far as possible) the continuity of Christian thought and expression. I believe that in very many cases the traditional language, when once its true meaning is known, will be found to be far more patient of a reasonable and a modern interpretation than is often supposed. It is, indeed, impossible that any educated person at the present day can really think of God and the universe exactly as was done by men of the fourth century or of the thirteenth or of the sixteenth.[14]

The atonement is particularly suited to this approach, for,

> The need for further study and bolder expression is here particularly pressing, and is perhaps more widely felt than in any other region. On the one hand, the idea that we are to be saved through Christ, and in some sense through His Cross, is much dearer to the hearts of most religious people than any technical presentation of the incarnation... On the other hand, there has been far more that is definitely irrational, repellent, and immoral in many theories of the atonement than there has been in any accepted theory of the incarnation. The revolt against these theories is, indeed, already pretty general; but the way to a healthier and more modern presentation is blocked by the surviving debris of shattered systems.[15]

Here we see the moral philosopher and social commentator criticizing theological systems which are incompatible with modern ideas of justice and fairness. Christian doctrine is not simply an abstract technical exercise hermetically sealed from our understanding of the world in general. It needs to form part of a more coherent and holistic world view:

> The question of the way in which human souls may be saved— that is to say, may attain to the highest ideal or true end of their

---

[14] Hastings Rashdall, *The Idea of Atonement in Christian Theology* (London: Macmillan & Co., 1919), p. vii.

[15] *Idea*, p. ix.

being—is obviously one which leads the enquirer at every turn into the profoundest questions of Moral Philosophy, of Psychology, and of Metaphysic. A full and complete philosophy of salvation would involve nothing less than a philosophy of the universe.[16]

In the lectures, Rashdall takes an historical and chronological approach to the understanding of the doctrine of the atonement. Starting with the teaching of Christ in the Gospels about forgiveness, he moves on to Pauline and other New Testament material before looking at patristic theories. A lecture is devoted to Augustine, Anselm, and Abelard, which leads to a discussion about the scholastic theology with which Rashdall had become familiar through his earlier work on the universities, focussing particularly on Aquinas. The penultimate lecture considers Luther and the Reformation, before Rashdall summarizes his findings in "The Truth of the Atonement", a positive restatement of the doctrine for modern times.

In this final chapter, Rashdall repeats his assertion that it is in Abelard that the subjective theory of the atonement receives its clearest expression:

> The most definite and systematic expression which this subjective view of the atonement has found is in the writings of Abelard and of those Schoolmen who wrote under his immediate influence. But it is, as we have seen, much older than Abelard. It represents, on the whole, in spite of the intrusion of some heterogeneous elements, the dominant view of the best Greek theology upon the subject, and pre-eminently of Origen.[17]

Rashdall hints at the ways in which the Abelardian view has been developed by Christian writers since the Reformation, from William Law and Coleridge to Bishop Westcott, before stating its formulation in the words of Peter Lombard:

---

[16] *Idea*, p. xii.
[17] *Idea*, p. 437.

> So great a pledge of love having been given us, we are both moved and kindled to love God who did such great things for us; and by this we are justified, that is, being loosed from our sins we are made just. The death of Christ therefore justifies us, inasmuch as through it charity is stirred up in our hearts.[18]

The battle is then taken to contemporary expressions of the penal substitutionary theory of the atonement, exemplified by the Scottish theologian, James Denney, whose books, *The Death of Christ* (1902) and *The Atonement and the Modern Mind* (1903), had mounted a forthright defence of the substitutionary view. Rashdall accuses Denney of taking a too narrow view of the efficacy of the death of Christ, seeing it as the whole of the saving work of Christ, rather than a necessary part of it. Here Rashdall is keen to align his views to the Catholic orthodoxy of Augustine and Aquinas, rather than either the one-sided theology of Lutheranism and Calvinism in this respect or the *de facto* Arianism—derived, he suggests, from Milton's *Paradise Lost*—of many ordinary Christians who have an inadequate understanding of the doctrine of the Trinity, supposing that God has three minds rather than one:

> We cannot think or talk of the atonement as involving any kind of transaction between the Father and the Son. The juridical, forensic view of the atonement has become impossible to modern thought, not merely because of the immoral or childish ideas of justice upon which it is based, but also because it treats the relation between the Father and the pre-existent Son as the relation between distinct juridical Persons, one of whom could offer and the other receive a sacrifice, one of whom could impose and the other endure a punishment.[19]

Having cleared away some mistaken views and misconceptions, Rashdall goes on to develop an understanding of the atonement founded on a degree Christology and the totality of the revelation of God in Christ,

---

[18] *Idea*, p. 438.

[19] *Idea*, pp. 445–6.

clearly drawing on his philosophical commitment to a morally centred and optimistic personal idealism:

> For most modern minds it will probably be found that the best and easiest way of translating the ancient patristic and scholastic thought about the divinity of Christ into present-day language is to think of the revelation of God in Christ as much as possible after the analogy of the imperfect but progressive revelation of God in other men—in the expanding developing mind of man, in the reason and conscience of the best men, and in their wills or characters, so far as they have conformed themselves to the ideal set up by conscience. If God and man are thought of—in the way which is sometimes called deistic—as two wholly separate and unlike kinds of being; or if (from a quite opposite point of view) God is thought of as a super-moral Absolute to whom we cannot attribute any of the moral qualities which are more or less recognized by the conscience of all men, and which are realized in the characters and lives of the best men and women, then indeed we could attach no meaning to the idea of an incarnation of God in one human being. But, if we can say that in humanity generally there is *some* revelation of God—a growing, developing, progressive revelation, and a higher degree of such a revelation in the heroes, the saints, the prophets, the founders and reformers of great religions, then the idea of an incarnation becomes possible. If we can say that God is to some extent revealed in all men, then it becomes possible to think of Him as making a supreme, culminating, unique revelation of Himself in one human character and life. And such a crowning revelation I believe that the conscience and reason of mankind do discover in the historical Jesus of Nazareth.[20]

This conceptual framework allows Rashdall to carry out his strategy of seeing the atonement in the light of the incarnation more generally. The two are inextricably linked and what we learn about the nature of God

---

[20] *Idea*, pp. 447–8.

from the incarnation will inform our understanding of the atonement. God does not—cannot in Rashdall's view—act against type.

Rashdall's approach soon brings him to the question of God's passibility—does God suffer on the cross? One is conscious of a degree of tension in Rashdall's grappling with this question. On the one hand, there is the meticulous recorder of Christian tradition: "I will only remind you that it is not orthodox to say that the divinity in Christ suffered ... But even in the West it has not been held orthodox to say that the Divine nature was 'passible' ... It is only in a very technical sense that the Church has allowed phrases which imply that God suffered or died."[21] On the other hand is the poignancy of a lecture delivered at a time when the First World War was raging, and making sense of suffering and the problem of evil was a pressing concern, and revised when the psychological and emotional impact of the war was still raw. Two of Rashdall's wife's brothers died in combat in 1915, shortly after the lectures had been delivered. That the tension remains unresolved is apparent from Rashdall's somewhat vague and evasive conclusion:

> We may not, without a pantheistic and unintelligible confusion between God and man or a Sabellian identification of one human mind with the supreme Mind of the universe, think of this or that man's pain as actually *being* the pain of the divine consciousness. We cannot think *that* even of Christ's sufferings; still less can we think of the eternal God as actually dying. So far the orthodox distinction is right. But we may reverently say that if God is good, if He is loving, if He looks upon men as His children—in a word, if He is like Christ—He *must* in some sense suffer in or with His creatures, and the more intensely in proportion to their nearness and dearness and likeness to Himself. A God who could contemplate such a world as ours without suffering would not be a loving God, nor would He be in the least like Christ. God must suffer with and in the sufferings of all His creatures.[22]

---

[21] *Idea*, pp. 450–1.

[22] *Idea*, pp. 452–3.

How, then, does the atonement work? How are we redeemed, if we have, to use Rashdall's words, "in the fullest and frankest manner given up all expiatory, transactional, or objective theories of redemption"?[23] By seeing the saving work of Christ as not confined simply to his death; by saying with, for instance, another Idealist, J. R. Illingworth, that the incarnation *is* the atonement:

> Christ's whole life was a sacrifice which takes away sin in the only way in which sin really can be taken away, and that is by making the sinner actually better. Much popular language on the subject has become quite unreal to ordinary modern minds, because it so completely isolates the death, or the sufferings which immediately preceded the death. The insistence of popular religious teaching upon the atoning efficacy of Christ's death loses all ethical value in proportion as it isolates and disconnects the atoning efficacy of that death from the saving influence of Christ's life, His teaching, His character, the visions of the risen Lord, and the hopes of immortality which those visions inspired.[24]

An implication of this approach is that human beings have a part to play in their salvation; they are not mere ciphers whose fate is decided in advance and who can have no influence on it. Christ's self-sacrifice,

---

[23] *Idea*, p. 454.

[24] *Idea*, pp. 454–5. J. R. Illingworth, *Reason and Revelation: An Essay in Christian Apology* (London: Macmillan, 1902), p. 228, writes of " ... the Incarnation in its atoning aspect". See also his essay, "The Incarnation in Relation to Development", in *Lux Mundi* (London: John Murray, 14th edition, 1895), pp. 132–57. At p. 133, Illingworth remarks on the tendency to privilege one doctrine over another: "Fragments of doctrine, torn from their context and deprived of their due proportions, are brandished in the eyes of men by well-meaning but ignorant apologists as containing the sum total of the Christian faith, with the lamentable consequence that even earnest seekers after truth, and much more its unearnest and merely factious adversaries, mislead themselves and others into thinking Christianity discredited, when in reality they have all along been criticising only its caricature."

"a death of suffering voluntarily submitted to from love of the brethren", is linked to his moral teaching, which "is not a code or a system, but the enunciation of a few great principles, principles which reveal a harmonious ideal, a character, a personality".[25] The real struggle for good against evil, which Rashdall outlined in his moral philosophy, is exemplified in those who follow Christ in a life of self-sacrifice:

> [I]t is only in the light of [Christ's] teaching about the love of God and the supreme place of love in the ethical ideal for man that the cross can be given its true meaning as the symbol of self-sacrifice—not of mere negative self-renunciation or self-denial for self-denial's sake, but of self-sacrifice inspired and directed by love of that moral ideal which is fully realized in God and by love of the men who are made in the image of God. It is because it is the typical expression of that spirit of self-sacrifice which dominated His life that the death of Christ has played, and will continue to play, a large part in its saving efficacy. When most of the theories about Christ's death have become obsolete and unintelligible, the cross will still be the symbol, known and understood by all, of this central feature in Christ's character and in the ideal for which He lived and died.[26]

Furthermore, that saving efficacy is inclusive. "If God be the sort of Being whose nature is best expressed by a self-sacrificing life and death, He could not have designed everlasting, meaningless, useless torments as the sole destiny in store for the great bulk of His creatures. That doctrine is dead..."[27] Although Rashdall is not a universalist, his ideal utilitarianism asserts itself in his belief that "the universe is realizing an end which is good not only on the whole but *for* the whole", for God cannot be "benevolent to humanity but unjust to vast numbers of individual human beings".[28]

---

[25] *Idea*, pp. 454, 456.
[26] *Idea*, p. 457.
[27] *Idea*, p. 458.
[28] *Idea*, p. 458.

Salvation for Rashdall is about "being saved from sin and becoming better: and goodness is an end in itself whether it is to last for a few years or for all eternity".[29] He believes that our life on earth is a "training-ground for a better and richer life of infinite possibilities beyond the grave, a place for the 'making of souls' ... ".[30] He concludes the book with a statement of the breadth of his understanding of salvation, which includes acknowledgement of the part played by folk or implicit religion:

> More and more, I believe, the great spiritual dividing line between men will be the line between those who really accept Christ's ideal of life and those who do not. Those who heartily believe in that ideal will probably in most cases find it possible to accept also Christ's outlook upon the universe as a universe controlled and guided by a conscious Will the nature and purpose of which may best be understood in the light of that same ideal. Those who believe that love is the thing of highest value in human life will generally believe also that "God is love indeed, and love Creation's highest law." But even if through intellectual perplexity they fail to do so, such persons may be placed among those of whom Christ said, "He that is not against us is for us," though they follow not with the great army of Christ's professed disciples. Many, doubtless, are being saved by this ideal who do not call themselves by Christ's name or formally associate themselves with those who do. And such men are in a very real sense being saved by Christ. And even among professing Christians by no means uninfluenced by the Christian ideal, there are probably millions whose highest spiritual life has been due more to the influence of the Christian community in which they have lived than to the conscious and deliberate following of Christ.[31]

Such a forthright and, at times, combative statement of the subjectivist view of the atonement was bound to divide theological opinion. Rashdall's

---

[29] *Idea*, p. 459.
[30] *Idea*, p. 459.
[31] *Idea*, pp. 463–4.

biographer hints at the mixed reaction the book received. Whilst there was widespread agreement on its significance—*The Spectator* described it as "one of the most important theological works that has appeared for more than a generation"—concerns were expressed about its incompleteness as a wholly adequate statement of Christian doctrine.[32] Charles Gore, unsurprisingly, was not impressed with it and, two years later, was to have a more serious clash with Rashdall over the divinity of Christ.

There is a sense in which *The Idea of Atonement in Christian Theology* was already an old-fashioned work by the time it was published. It is very rarely, if ever, that intellectual movements are killed stone dead, but among the effects of the First World War on philosophical and theological thought in the West, the idealist tradition appeared to have been dealt a devastating blow. Its optimistic and progressive notes, already criticized from within the academic fold, rang falsely in a world which had been devastated. Amid all that was broken, systematic theories of the universe had no place. It is instructive to reflect that, almost contemporaneously with Rashdall, Karl Barth was working on his first great book, *The Epistle to the Romans*. This repudiation of the German liberal protestant tradition in which Barth had been formed was started in 1916 and published in 1919, the same year as *The Idea of the Atonement*, with a revised edition in 1922.

Theology was taking a conservative turn. Reflecting on his experience of moving to Paris in 1924, Nicolai Berdyaev, the Russian Orthodox theologian, wrote:

> My impressions among the Western Christians, both Catholic and Protestant, were in some measure similar to those I had among the Russian Christians. They too appeared to me to a great extent in the grip of religious reaction ... This reaction took the form of a "return", a going back to all kinds of things, in search of stable authority and tradition amidst the uncertainties

---

[32] Matheson, pp. 192–3.

of human existence. This was particularly evident among the neo-Thomists and neo-Calvinists.[33]

In 1929, in the foreword to a collection of essays edited by L. W. Grensted, *The Atonement in History and in Life*, the Bishop of Chelmsford, Henry Wilson, acknowledged Rashdall's contribution to stimulating a moderately conservative reassessment of the doctrine of the atonement in the Anglican church:

> The doctrine of the Atonement has always been a subject upon which widely divergent opinions have been held in the Christian Church. It is probably true to say that the opinion of scholars in recent years has definitely inclined in the direction of those theories of the doctrine which may roughly be called "subjective." Beyond doubt, this has been in considerable measure the outcome of that impressive work of the late Dean Hastings Rashdall: *The Idea of Atonement in Christian Theology*.
>
> Nevertheless, there are, and always have been, competent authorities who are by no means prepared to regard all that is commonly understood as the "objective" side of the Atonement as a mere example of crude thinking or as a survival of pre-Christian or sub-Christian religion. The very fact of this survival seems to testify to the existence of a core of truth, overlaid, it may be, by bad and even repellent forensic theories.
>
> This volume of essays arose from the dissatisfaction which a group of friends felt at the unceremonious way in which, so it seemed to them, the whole Anselmian view, which had become popularized in the Evangelical movement of the last century, . . . had been tossed aside as finally disproved and discredited.[34]

---

[33] Nicolai Berdyaev, *Dream and Reality: An Essay in Autobiography*, tr. Katherine Lampert (London: Geoffrey Bless, 1950), p. 258.

[34] L. W. Grensted (ed.), *The Atonement in History and in Life* (London: SPCK, 1929), p. 1.

Two years later the Swedish theologian, Gustaf Aulén, published his classic work, *Christus Victor: An Historical Study of the Three Main Types of the Idea of Atonement*. Aulén considers Rashdall, along with Schleiermacher and Ritschl, as an example of the subjective or humanistic type of atonement theory, and exposes what he thought to be its inadequacies:

> No doubt Rashdall may be regarded as comparing favourably with Continental theologians of a similar tendency, in so far as he follows the praiseworthy English tradition in giving a greater place to the Incarnation than the German writers whom we have discussed. Nevertheless, it cannot be said that he gives adequate expression to the Christian idea of the Incarnation; like other idealistic writers, he allows the highest human to shade off into the Divine, and thus obscures the distinction between the Divine and the human. Christ reveals God, because He exhibits the ideal manhood ... But it is particularly important to see that the question of Salvation is treated by him just as much from the ethical point of view as by Schleiermacher ... The weakness of this exposition is not to be found in the language about the ethical effects of the Divine forgiveness on human lives; on the contrary, this is its strength. Its weakness is that the forgiving and atoning work of God is *made dependent upon* the ethical effects in human lives; consequently, the Divine Love is not clearly set forth as a free spontaneous love. Wherever there is such a view of the Divine Love, as not called forth by the worthiness or goodness of men, but bestowing value on men by the very fact that they are loved by God, the work of the Divine forgiveness always appears as prior to ethical regeneration, not dependent upon or proportioned to human repentance or any other conditions on man's side.[35]

---

[35] Gustaf Aulén, *Christus Victor: An Historical Study of the Three Main Types of the Idea of Atonement*, tr. A. G. Hebert (London, SPCK, 1934), pp. 139–40.

It would be interesting to speculate how Rashdall, had he lived, would have responded to these criticisms. His projected study of the incarnation would have provided him with the opportunity. At the time of the book's publication, however, he acknowledged to a correspondent that none of the hostile reviewers had seriously misrepresented him.[36] It may simply be the case that the matter is not conducive to rational explanation but requires the admixture of religious feeling which Rashdall's critics were quick to point out he had omitted from his account. This was the somewhat wistful conclusion of F. R. Barry, by then the retired Bishop of Southwell, looking back in 1974 at the vicissitudes of the liberal theology for which he had been a distinguished advocate:

> Liberal Protestantism has regarded it [the subjective theory] as the one tenable theory of the Atonement, evangelical, ethical and truly Christian, and "entirely in harmony", as Rashdall claims, "with the earlier traditions of the Church"... Few Christians will fail to be attracted by it; yet it does not seem possible to claim for it that it has any real Scriptural authority.[37]

William Temple, personally indebted to Rashdall in so many ways, was more forthright in his criticism in correspondence after Rashdall's death than he had been in his public comments at the time of the

---

[36] Matheson, p. 193.

[37] F. R. Barry, *The Atonement* (London: Hodder & Stoughton, 1968), p. 147. In the same year, in his inaugural lecture at King's College London, "Looking into the Sun", Maurice Wiles made a similar general point: "Accounts of the incarnation based on the analogy of our human experience of divine grace from Theodore of Mopsuestia to Donald Baillie, so-called 'subjective' theories of the atonement from Abelard to Hastings Rashdall, have had a strong appeal as providing intellectually intelligible and religiously attractive accounts of Christ and of his work; yet as statements of Christian doctrine they have generally been dubbed inadequate on the one ground of their failure to do justice to the radical distinctness of Christ's person and to the objective character of his work." Maurice Wiles, *Working Papers in Doctrine* (London: SCM Press, 1976), p. 155.

book's publication. Writing to Bishop E. W. Barnes of Birmingham, a redoubtable modernist, in 1930, Temple commented:

> I regard Rashdall's book on the Atonement as a great achievement, but essentially a bad piece of theology—because when he has decided that some Pauline or Augustinian computation is untenable he never stops to enquire why S. Paul or S. Augustine *wanted* to hold it, what spiritual value it had for them: he omits from his study the very thing that matters most. And that seems to me typical of so many Modernist utterances.[38]

Temple's comments exemplify a consistent theme in the criticism of Rashdall's theological stance; his apparent inability, or unwillingness, to give sufficient weight to the claims of religious experience as a guide to truth. Similar comments made by observers as varied as Rashdall's sister and von Hügel have already been noted, as well as Rashdall's own scepticism about the value of Christian mysticism and his critique of

---

[38] F. A. Iremonger, *William Temple, Archbishop of Canterbury: His Life and Letters* (London: Oxford University Press, 1948), pp. 491–2. Ernest William Barnes (1874–1953) was perhaps the most controversial English bishop of his time, in quite a competitive field. A brilliant mathematician (the Barnes integral is still discussed in the mathematical literature), he became a Fellow of Trinity College, Cambridge and was elected a Fellow of the Royal Society in 1909. Already ordained in 1902, he devoted the rest of his life to public ministry, as Master of the Temple in 1915 and then a Canon of Westminster Abbey before becoming Ramsay MacDonald's first, and controversial, episcopal appointment in 1924 as Bishop of Birmingham, where he remained until his retirement in 1953. He attracted attention as a scourge of Anglo-Catholicism in his diocese, a convinced pacifist and eugenicist, and the author of modernist works such as *The Rise of Christianity* (1947), which questioned the doctrines of the virgin birth and the bodily resurrection of Christ. Such headline-grabbing stances inevitably deflected attention from his careful work as a diocesan bishop, particularly in the rebuilding of the church, both physically and spiritually, after the devastation of the Second World War.

religious experience as a concept which provides reliable access to truth. Looking back on Rashdall's work, Clement Webb identified personal consciousness—"the absolute, unqualified reality of individual persons, minds, or spirits"—as the key to understanding his theology. One consequence of this was that:

> He always regarded with suspicion the attempts now [Webb was writing in 1928] so often made to rest belief in God on "religious experience". He professed himself to be entirely a stranger to any "experience" which could be fairly described as an "immediate" consciousness of the Divine Being; nor did he consider that any such "immediate" consciousness was a necessary condition of the practice of worship and prayer... Holding, as he always did, that the knowledge which each of us has of other minds than his own is purely inferential, he naturally regarded the inferential character of our belief in God as no more a bar to intercourse with Him than the no less inferential character of our belief in the reality of our friends is a bar to that which we enjoy with them.[39]

Webb also noted that Rashdall "never found it easy to enter with intellectual sympathy into positions widely different from his own".[40] It is fair to say that Rashdall's stress on a particular intellectual foundation for his theology (personal Idealism), his insistence on the priority of its ethical dimension, his denigration of religious experience, and his combative approach to opposing viewpoints, born perhaps of a lack of empathy for what others were trying to achieve (or possibly what they believed), gave a hard edge to his theological writing which engenders respect rather than enthusiastic support. When he was in full flow against an uncongenial opponent or viewpoint, he could be very amusing. His 1913 review of Wilfrid Ward's *Life* of Cardinal Newman, for example, twits the zeal of the new convert: "his belief in the Pope personally as always guided by the Holy Spirit even in his non-infallible utterances

---

[39] C. C. J. Webb, "Rashdall as Philosopher and Theologian", in Matheson, pp. 240, 243.

[40] *Ibid.*, p. 245.

wore off to some extent with further experience of the actual Pontiff and the wretched crew with which he was surrounded". And he finishes with a dig against his own Anglican opponents: "The book from beginning to end is a commentary on the value of that religious liberty—liberty for priests as well as for laymen—of which the High Anglicans have availed themselves so amply, however anxious they may be to deny it to others."[41] But he could go too far. A colleague, probably Webb himself, commenting on one of Rashdall's drafts, advised him to tone down an attack on Gore: "But don't you think you could minimise a little, or omit, or at least soften, the carping references to Gore? People will begin to get rather to expect them, soon, & that would be a pity."[42]

It was this passionate and combative approach that Rashdall brought to another dimension of his theological enterprise, his role as a public theologian, seeking to make a difference in thought and action, and, in his eyes, to promote good in the battle against evil, the purer truth against the second-rate.

---

[41] *Ideas and Ideals*, pp. 123–4, 131.
[42] Bodl. Lib., R. H. MSS., RH 110, no. 25, MS comments on undated paper by Rashdall.

6

Pursuing good and resisting evil: Rashdall's theology in practice

Although he published substantial works of scholarship in history, philosophy, and theology, Rashdall was no armchair academic, hermetically sealed from the world around him. The impact and influence of such work is, in any case, liable to take time to take root and grow. For all those who knew and valued Rashdall's work for its careful and measured scholarship, there were many more for whom he was an enthusiastic and sometimes pugnacious promoter of causes, who enjoyed the cut and thrust of debate and was indefatigable in his engagement with it. The bibliography of his published works runs to over 400 items, from books and scholarly articles to lectures, sermons, book reviews, and letters to newspapers, both local and national. He lived, of course, at a time when the printed word was the primary medium of communication beyond the very local but, even so, this was an impressive output. It would be a daunting task to provide an exhaustive categorization and analysis of this material, particularly as much of it is addressed to debates and controversies which now only have an antiquarian interest. There are, however, themes which are consistent throughout his life. These include a passionate concern about how the Christian life is actually lived out, especially in its social, economic, and political aspects—the concept of justice and the crafting of a renewed form of casuistry were particularly important for him here; the promotion of a liberal understanding of theology which took seriously modern critical thinking and allowed clergy, in particular, greater freedom in their interpretation and explanation of the Christian faith; an interest, as a result of this, in clerical education and training; and an ecumenical cast of mind which led him to foster good working relationships with other Christian churches. His work on the medieval universities had also given him an interest, and considerable background knowledge, in the matter of university reform and wider access, particularly for women, which was the subject of lively debate in his day.

Rashdall as a public theologian: politics and society

Rashdall's public theology was not formed in a vacuum. As well as the lively exchange of views in print, his was an age of a vigorous conversational approach to the advancement of understanding. This could be quite informal. Like many Oxford tutors of his generation, Rashdall organized reading parties for undergraduates during vacations, and held fortnightly meetings of academics and favoured students in his rooms in New College to discuss theology and philosophy. Sometimes gatherings were more focussed and intentional, structured discussions which resulted in the publication of collections of essays—*Lux Mundi*, *Foundations*, and *Personal Idealism* are examples of this approach. The Synthetic Society, a London-based group founded by A. J. Balfour, Wilfrid Ward, Charles Gore, and others in 1896, provided an opportunity for some of the leading thinkers of the day to meet regularly, monthly for the first five months of the year, "to consider existing agnostic tendencies, and to contribute towards a working philosophy of religious belief". Rashdall was an early member and contributed three papers. And, finally, there was a plethora of organizations, societies, and committees to discuss particular issues or motivate support for particular causes. Rashdall played a leading part in two of these organizations, the Christian Social Union (CSU), which he joined at its formation in 1889 and became joint editor of the Oxford University branch's journal, the *Economic Review*, in 1892, and the Churchmen's Union for the Advancement of Liberal Religious Thought (later the Modern Churchmen's Union), of which he became the founding vice-president in 1898. Both these organizations gave him a platform for the dissemination of his ideas, particularly through their journals, as well as a forum for debate. He also became a member of the Church of England Peace League and of The Group, which gathered round B. H. Streeter, the Oxford theologian and later colleague of Rashdall in Hereford.

Through his involvement with the CSU, Rashdall had the opportunity to give wider circulation to ideas which we have noted already. Against absolute Idealists such as Bradley and Bosanquet, he wanted to assert the importance of the individual's responsibility to pursue the good, rather than being absorbed in the common good, or general will, of society seen as a social organism. To those within the Church who, then as now, criticized the Church's involvement in debates about politics and social ethics, he attempted to counter the way in which such critics were prone to use biblical or historical references to support their view without considering either their context or the way in which moral thinking needed to develop in response to actual situations. Scriptural material can rarely be translated in a straightforward way into the solving of moral dilemmas.

In 1896, soon after taking up his post at New College, Rashdall gave a series of lectures to the London branch of the CSU, which were published in the *Economic Review* and also in pamphlet form. In her analysis of Rashdall's role in the renewal of Christian social ethics, Jane Garnett has written of these lectures:

> "The Rights of the State", "The Rights of the Church" and "The Rights of the Individual" established his general principle that moral judgements must rest not on *a priori* justifications, but on the whole social context of action. These lectures aimed to provide an important framework for CSU activity, and to begin to analyse the criteria by which to define the parameters of the good life.[1]

In the lecture on the state, Rashdall deploys the ideal utilitarian approach on which he was working for *The Theory of Good and Evil* to examine

---

[1] Jane Garnett, "Hastings Rashdall and the Renewal of Christian Social Ethics, c.1890–1920", in Jane Garnett and Colin Matthew (eds), *Revival and Religion since 1700: Essays for John Walsh* (London and Rio Grande, OH: Hambledon Press, 1993), p. 308. The lecture is reproduced in *Ideas and Ideals*, pp. 22–39.

the concept of political obedience and to criticize the way in which generalizations about the social organism and the general will had sucked the meaning out of individual moral action:

> The social organism... threatens to become as unintelligible a catchword as the rights of man. The idea is true enough in its way, but the phrase is in danger of serving as a mere substitute for thought... Merely to tell a man that he is part of the social organism supplies him with no reason for becoming a martyr or even a decently good citizen.[2]

For Rashdall political obedience must be related to the end which government serves. This is not simply pleasure—the greatest happiness of the greatest number—, although pleasure is a part of human good, but intellectual activity, goodness, and virtue. Although the state cannot remain indifferent to religion, this view does not determine the nature of the relationship between church and state, any more than it prescribes a particular view of the state towards matters of morality, education, or social organization. These can only be addressed in a more detailed and contextual way through the application of principles to particular circumstances.

In the lecture on the Church, Rashdall expressed his strong conviction that it was impossible to divide life into two mutually exclusive spheres—the sacred and the secular. In the same way, church and state cannot be separated either, although this did not lead him to a strongly Erastian view of the established Church, arguing that while the state is compulsive, the church is essentially voluntary. He used this as the basis for arguing, for example, for non-denominational education as providing the greatest good, because it promoted the real interests of education itself, rather than particular sectional interests.[3]

---

[2] Garnett, "Hastings Rashdall and the Renewal of Christian Social Ethics", p. 308.

[3] Garnett, "Hastings Rashdall and the Renewal of Christian Social Ethics", p. 309. The lecture is printed in *Ideas and Ideals*, pp. 40–58.

His lecture on the rights of the individual in relation to the state resolved that there were two of them—the right to life and the right to equality of consideration. He dismissed equality of opportunity as impractical. This was because of the impossibility of achieving this in a uniform way (for example, relating an increase in educational opportunities to an increase in the employment and professional opportunities which would need to follow) without curtailing individual freedoms which it is the state's duty to uphold. We see here a consistency with the views on the freedom of the individual which Rashdall expressed in his moral philosophy.[4]

In September of the same year, 1896, Rashdall preached at a service in Edinburgh to mark the annual meeting of the Trades Union Congress. Taking as his text Mark 1:14-15, Jesus's declaration of the coming of the kingdom of God, he used the occasion to sketch out the aims of the CSU and the principles on which it was based, stating that:

> ... the CSU is not committed to any definite policy about social questions ... But there are some things about which we are all agreed. About means we differ: about principles we are all agreed.

These included a conviction that:

> ... [t]he teaching of Christ is meant to regulate the whole of our social and public life—domestic politics and foreign policy, trade and local government—as well as our private life and individual conduct. Therefore we hold that it is a duty to endeavour to apply these Christian principles to all parts of our social life—in voting at elections, in politics or in local government, in questions of buying and selling and investing and employing labour, and so on.

However:

---

[4] Garnett, "Hastings Rashdall and the Renewal of Christian Social Ethics", p. 309; *Ideas and Ideals*, pp. 59-77.

> Social questions are difficult questions. They require thought and study as well as zeal and activity. Social problems cannot be solved by a kind heart... the business of the wise is to undo the harm that has been done by the good.

Pressing home his point with his trades unionist audience in mind, Rashdall concluded:

> And here is one serious result of study—one result which nobody who thinks seriously about social questions can help coming to. When we discover how wealth is really made, how all wealth is truly the result of labour (if you only have a wide enough conception of what labour is) we cannot help looking upon all our wealth—whether it comes from interest in investments or from an official salary or from profits of trade or from weekly wages—as so much pay given us by the Community for work done.

Hence the need for a fair share of work for the wages we receive. Hence, too, the inevitability of the uneven distribution of wealth:

> We want to get to look upon idleness, whether in rich or in poor, in exactly the same light which in we all look upon stealing. We have no right to take the pay without doing the work.[5]

Given his acute awareness of historical context and moral complexity, together with his impatience with people reading into the Bible things that aren't there, it is not surprising that Rashdall had little time for ideological politics or ideological religion, in the sense of choosing between competing absolutes. He was himself a Liberal by political persuasion—another of Montagu Butler's legacies—and a supporter of causes such as women's suffrage.[6] But he could be sharply critical of

---

[5] Bodl. Lib., R. H. MSS., Box 109, No. 15, fols 10–12.

[6] In her *ODNB* article, Jane Garnett categorizes Rashdall more specifically as a Liberal who was inclined to unionism, being late to accept Irish Home

those on either side of him. In 1913, he criticized Bosanquet's apologia for capitalism as being too one-sided, while earlier, in 1908, he had a sharp exchange with the young and enthusiastic William Temple, who had published an article, "The Church and the Labour Party", in the *Economic Review*, in which he argued that "there is no middle way between the acceptance of socialism and the declaration that the gospel cannot be applied to economics". Rashdall's response in the same issue, "Is the Christian Necessarily a Socialist?", gave a firmly negative answer, accusing Temple of being both acutely unhistorical and muddled in his thinking. It made no sense, in Rashdall's view, to identify the gospel with any specific form of social organization. He was also annoyed with Temple for exposing the CSU to precisely the kind of attack from critics such as Inge and Henson from which he, Rashdall, had been working so strenuously to defend it.[7]

—

Rashdall's perception of the dangers inherent in the absolute idealist theory of the state put forward by writers such as Bosanquet reached an acute form at the time of the First World War, when it became clear to him and others that Germany had pursued an absolutist state ideology which put the state above morality and placed the national interest above all other considerations. In his contribution to a series of lectures published as *The International Crisis: The Theory of the State* in 1916, Rashdall commented on:

> the irrationality and internal contradiction involved in the doctrine that Germany or any other nation is justified in making its own good the only rule for its internal or external policy. The subordination of one nation's interests to those of the whole

---

Rule and remaining a decided opponent of the disestablishment of the Welsh church. Prichard states: "... [T]hough an ardent Liberal, he gave the impression of belonging to an earlier generation." H. A. P[richard]., "Dr. Hastings Rashdall", *Hertford College Magazine* 13 (April 1924), p. 6.

[7] See Garnett, *art. cit.*, for a discussion of the exchange with Temple.

world is as manifest a dictate of reason as the individual's duty to subordinate his own interests to the welfare of his particular state.[8]

He commented further, in another lecture on the war:

> The criminal nation surely must be punished much as the criminal individual. There is nothing inconsistent with Christian love in desiring to punish Germany for her offences against the commonwealth of nations. The interests of humanity certainly require that Germany and its rulers should somehow be punished—that it should be made plain for all time that undisguised greed of power and of gain, contempt for international agreements, disregard of the commonest instincts of humanity and justice do not in the long-run pay.[9]

In a sermon on "International Immoralism", undated but likely to have been preached at about the same time, Rashdall had spelled out the dangerous influence of Nietzsche and his Prussian followers, Treitschke and Bernhardi:

> I daresay you have already heard many sermons directed against the philosophy or pseudo-philosophy and the Ethics which are so largely responsible for the present war and all the untold suffering which it has brought with it.

He goes on:

> It is characteristic of the German mind that it cannot do things without a theory. It is not content with imitating, by its own

---

[8] Quoted by Matthew Grimley, *Citizenship, Community, and the Church of England: Liberal Anglican Theories of the State between the Wars* (Oxford: Clarendon Press, 2004), p. 61.

[9] Bodl. Lib., R. H. MSS., RH 111, undated typescript.

confession, the foreign policy and military methods of Attila. It must find a defence for its conduct in a theory.

Rashdall then outlines the theory, as expressed by the Prussian military thinker, Bernhardi:

1. The German State is the highest State in the world.
2. It is in the highest interests of Germany to exercise the highest domination.
3. It is good for the rest of the world that this domination should be exercised.

Rashdall concludes this striking sermon:

> If I were inclined to trace the present war to the defects of Teutonic Religion, I should trace it rather to the fact that German Protestantism—whether liberal or orthodox—has a strong tendency to exalt a vague religious sentimentality above both reason and morality.[10]

The characteristic Rashdall concern for the application of clear theological thinking to issues of morality and human flourishing, in contrast to emotional responses, is once more apparent. It was carried through in his practical support for the war effort, from welcoming Belgian refugees into his house in Hereford, to working for naval intelligence later in the war.[11]

---

[10] Pusey House, Rashdall MSS., HRA B5, no. 9, fols 1–15.

[11] Rashdall wrote to his mother in December 1914 about the arrival of a Belgian couple, the man a journalist on *Le Soir*, a leading Brussels newspaper: "They are quite nice people. But Madame has not much notion of amusing herself, and Connie has to talk to her by the hour, which she does with marvellous vivacity, in spite of a somewhat limited French vocabulary. I am bound to say that it is a little burdensome ... " New Coll., PA/RAS, 6/1, Rashdall to E. M. Rashdall, The Residence, 16 December 1914. Matheson tells us that

Rashdall as a public theologian: Apologetics in the modern world

Throughout his career Rashdall was a staunch proponent of the necessity of relating the Christian faith to modern thinking and experience, and most of his theological work was done with this in mind. Because he was also keen to defend the rights of individuals to consider these matters for themselves, rather than accepting them on the basis of some external authority such as the Bible and the Church, he was drawn inevitably into discussions about the freedom allowable to the clergy to dissent from, or cast doubt on, certain traditional doctrines. At the time, all clergy of the Church of England were required to declare their assent specifically and in full to the Thirty-Nine Articles of Religion as the nearest thing the Church had to a statement of faith or confession. The declaration also included a statement of the place of scripture and the historic creeds of the Church as the foundation of Christian doctrine. This declaration, or subscription, as it was known, had until recently also been required of those who had been appointed to other offices, such as fellows of Oxford and Cambridge colleges.

Rashdall's first significant public foray into this debate was carried out somewhat reluctantly, and against an opponent whom he greatly admired. In 1896, Henry Sidgwick, the professor of moral philosophy at Cambridge whose work was an important influence on Rashdall's own thinking in this area, published in *The International Journal of Ethics* an address he had given to the West London Ethical Society—founded by Stanton Coit in 1891 as one of a number of such societies aimed at gathering people who were interested in exploring moral issues outside a specifically religious framework—on the ethics of religious conformity and, in particular, the matter of clerical subscription. This was something in which Sidgwick had a personal interest. In 1869, he had resigned from his fellowship at Trinity College, Cambridge because he could no longer think of himself as a member of the Church of England, and could not, in conscience, subscribe to the Thirty-Nine Articles. He, therefore, in a

---

they were the de Joncks and stayed with the Rashdalls for four months in Hereford and Oxford (Matheson, p. 155).

very principled way, took the hardline view that all Church of England clergy had an obligation to accept a literal interpretation of the creeds, otherwise they were breaking a solemn pledge, and their good faith was called into question. Sidgwick saw this strict requirement as being "an inexorable moral barrier" to any efforts to liberalize the teaching of the Church of England. For laypeople, he thought that there was an implicit obligation in the baptismal promises taken by them, or on their behalf, to believe the articles of the Apostles' Creed, although he admitted that the requirement for a literal interpretation might legitimately be relaxed. In his consideration of the relationship between Christian doctrine and modern thought, he unerringly identified miracles, and particularly the doctrine of the virgin birth, as points of challenge and incompatibility. It was doubt about the virgin birth which was shortly to cause William Temple agonies of indecision as he approached his ordination, and Rashdall was one of those to whom he turned for advice.[12]

Rashdall was asked by the editors of the journal to reply, and he did so with some reluctance and trepidation:

> To those who are anxious to maintain the comprehensiveness of the Church of England by a liberal interpretation of its formulae, it must be a matter of profound regret that the judgment of a man such as Professor Sidgwick should be on the whole against them. The fact that such an article has appeared seems to make it desirable that some one who believes in the possibility of combining honesty with a considerable measure of theological liberalism within the limits of the Church of England should attempt some kind of apology for his position.[13]

His defence was a characteristic amalgam of principle and practicality. The starting point was an appeal to the reality of the situation, that members of all parties in the Church are constantly giving their assent

---

[12] Matheson, pp. 86–7; G. L. Prestige, *The Life of Charles Gore, a Great Englishman* (London: William Heinemann, 1935), pp. 192–3.

[13] "Professor Sidgwick on the Ethics of Religious Conformity: A Reply", *International Journal of Ethics* VII (1896–7), pp. 137–68, quotation at p. 138.

to things they do not believe and which they are known not to believe. This might not be an ideal state of affairs, but it is inevitable, given the impossibility of articulating Christian belief in precise formulae. Further, Rashdall thought that a distinction cannot be drawn between assent to an obsolete Article and assent to a detail of the creed, provided that this is not essential to a belief in the incarnation and the unique revelation in Jesus Christ. In other words, the same latitude should be allowed in the interpretation of the creeds as would normally be given to the interpretation of the Articles. Finally, there is the appeal to the idea of development in doctrine. The vital force which is necessary for the life of the Church can only be maintained by the reinterpretation of the traditional Christian formulae from age to age. On Sidgwick's specific point about the doctrine of the virgin birth, Rashdall pointed out that it was not in the original creed of Nicaea and held that it was not essential to the doctrine of the incarnation.[14]

The views expressed in his response to Sidgwick remained Rashdall's settled position on the matter. They were not uniformly welcomed, and there were significant dissenting voices, most prominently Charles Gore, a fellow Harrovian, who wrote to Rashdall to protest. It was the first significant public difference of opinion between the two men and marked the beginning of a wider divergence, culminating in stormy exchanges of views in the 1920s.[15]

---

[14] Matheson, p. 87.

[15] Charles Gore (1853–1932) left Harrow the term before Rashdall arrived, to go to the Balliol College of Benjamin Jowett and T. H. Green, where he excelled academically as well as developing a keen interest in social justice, reflecting the influence of both Green and B. F. Westcott, who taught him at Harrow, and leading him to be one of the co-founders of the Christian Social Union. Academic posts in Oxford followed, including becoming the first Principal of Pusey House in 1884 and Bampton Lecturer in 1891: he also found time to start the Community of the Resurrection. The year 1894 saw his move to a wider national prominence as a canon at Westminster Abbey, followed by a rapid succession of bishoprics—Worcester (1902), Birmingham (1905), and Oxford (1911), where he stayed until his retirement in 1919. Towards the end of his life, he was appointed Gifford Lecturer (1929–30). Always a

This last passage of arms with Gore was occasioned by the annual conference of the Churchmen's Union at Girton College, Cambridge in 1921. Rashdall had been a strong supporter of the union from its foundation in 1898. He had served as vice-president from the beginning and became president in the last year of his life. He contributed to the union's journal, *The Modern Churchman*, and was a regular speaker at the annual conferences, which started in 1914.

The subject of the Girton conference in 1921 was "Christ and the Creeds". Rashdall read a paper on "Christ as Logos and Son of God". Nothing he said would have been startling or unfamiliar to those who had read his published theological work over more than 20 years. He began by making five points:

1. Jesus did not claim Divinity for Himself.
2. Jesus was in the fullest sense man.
3. It is unorthodox to suppose that the human soul pre-existed.
4. The Divinity of Christ does not necessarily imply the Virgin Birth or any other miracle.
5. The Divinity of Christ does not imply omniscience.

He went on to maintain that we must believe that every human soul incarnates God to a certain extent, but that in Christ we see the fullest disclosure of God in humanity:

---

convinced catholic and sacramentalist, as a young theologian Gore was keen to incorporate the findings of biblical criticism and scientific knowledge, such that his editorship of the volume *Lux Mundi* in 1889 drew criticism from some of his fellow catholics for its liberal approach. At this time, Gore and Rashdall saw a fair amount of each other in Oxford and were on good personal terms. Their "unfortunate antagonism", to use the description of Gore's biographer (see Prestige, *op. cit.*, p. 196), with its tendency to invite misunderstandings and misrepresentations, dated from the time of the Sidgwick controversy, when both men had moved to more public positions as leaders of different points of view in the Church of England, refusing to compromise what each saw as the truth of the matter and choosing to accentuate their differences rather than build on what they had in common.

> If we believe that every human soul reveals, reproduces, incarnates God *to some extent*; if we believe that in the great ethical teachers of mankind, the great religious personalities, the founders, the reformers of religions, the heroes, the prophets, the saints, God is more fully revealed than in other men: if we believe that up to the coming of Christ there had been a gradual, continuous, and on the whole progressive manifestation of God (especially, though by no means exclusively, in the development of Jewish Monotheism), then it becomes possible to believe that in one Man the self-revelation of God has been signal, supreme, unique. That we are justified in thinking of God as like Christ, that the character and teaching of Christ contains the fullest disclosure both of the character of God Himself and of His will for man—that is (so far as so momentous a truth can be summed up in a few words) the true meaning for us of the doctrine of Christ's Divinity.[16]

In conclusion, Rashdall commented on the Logos doctrine, favouring the ideas of Augustine and Aquinas against the claim by some patristic writers that the Logos is a separate consciousness of Deity.

Rashdall's paper, and another by J. F. Bethune-Baker, on "Jesus as both Human and Divine", caused a storm of protest which is hard to imagine or understand today. This happened immediately—national newspapers published reports and comment on the conference—and was intensified when the conference papers were published, as was the custom, in a special issue of *The Modern Churchman*. Some of the reaction was the instinctive and often misinformed response of traditionally minded Christians to what they saw as the undermining of the faith. There were articles and letters to the press; there were even demands that Rashdall and others should be tried for heresy. A writer in the *Sunday Pictorial* a week after the conference had ended suggested: "There are some of

---

[16] *God and Man*, p. 74. For a discussion of the Girton conference and its background, see A. M. G. Stephenson, *The Rise and Decline of English Modernism (The Hulsean Lectures 1979–80)* (London: SPCK, 1984), pp. 99–122.

us still left who believe in the divinity of Christ, and who totally fail to understand how men who believe the contrary can honestly occupy the pulpits of our State churches and take money for teaching people to deride the ancient faith."[17] Charles Gore was not slow to launch an attack in the *Star*:

> I feel sure that the denial of miracles and the abandonment of belief in Christ's Godhead will be found to bring with them an abandonment of Divine Revelation altogether, and those who abandon the specific Christian Creed will find themselves not in the Unitarianism of Dr Martineau, but much lower down.[18]

Nor did Rashdall hold back in his response to criticisms which he regarded as ignorant and unwarranted, claiming that "My paper distinctly asserted the Divinity of Christ. All my philosophical writings are a protest against Modern Pantheism and strongly defend the Personality of God."[19] He also had a more measured public debate with Gore in a series of articles in 1921 and 1922, particularly focussing on Athanasius and Aquinas and their handling of the doctrines of the incarnation, Logos, and Trinity. Rashdall's close acquaintance with Aquinas, dating back to his work on the medieval universities and reinforced by his reading for the Bampton Lectures, won the approval of the Dominican theologian, Vincent McNabb, who noted somewhat gleefully in *Blackfriars*, "The Bishop does not really seem as acquainted with the orthodox Trinitarian doctrine as does the Dean!"[20]

The aftermath of the Girton conference revealed both the breadth of theological opinion in the Church of England and the reputational

---

[17] Stephenson, *The Rise and Decline of English Modernism*, p. 123.
[18] Stephenson, *The Rise and Decline of English Modernism*, p. 123. James Martineau (1805-1900) was the leading Unitarian thinker of his generation. Much respected outside his own denomination, he was Principal of Manchester College, Oxford for many years.
[19] Stephenson, *The Rise and Decline of English Modernism*, p. 123.
[20] Vincent McNabb, "Bishop Gore, Dean Rashdall and St Thomas Aquinas", *Blackfriars* III:30, p. 356.

damage caused by the vituperative way in which it was discussed in public.[21] At times, protagonists appeared more interested in scoring political points on behalf of their part of the Church than engaging in serious theological discussion. In any case, the public prints are hardly ever the best medium for debating issues which turn on nuances of language and interpretation and it was, perhaps, naïve of Rashdall and his supporters and opponents not to realize this. One result of the theological ferment was the decision made, somewhat reluctantly, by the Archbishop of Canterbury, Randall Davidson, at the end of 1922 to set up a Doctrine Commission. Rashdall declined to serve on it, as he did not think it was a good idea. It is some indication of the complexities of the issues with which it was dealing that the Commission did not produce its report until 1938. Adrian Hastings, the historian of English Christianity in the period, described it as "a pondered, rather dull document, as was inevitable given the drawn-out circumstances and varied views of its producers... most of [it] is—for the late 1930s—rather anachronistically liberal and modernist. It decided nothing, stimulated little."[22] The theological tide had turned, and the prospect of another world war was turning attention to other matters.

Rashdall's engagement with the Modern Churchmen's Union raises the question of what might be called the liberal dilemma. What is the best way of encouraging greater openness in debate and the consideration of new ideas and fresh interpretations? Is it by setting up an organization to promote them, which can easily turn into a pressure group which

---

[21] It has recently been suggested that the Girton conference marked a turning point in the ecclesiastical politics of the Church of England, with Gore and others successfully manoeuvring a liberal expression of Christian doctrine into something of a cul-de-sac, as expressing the views of one particular party or faction within the Church, rather than a theological method to be used by the Church as a whole. Rashdall's own fear of "liberal Christianity" becoming a separate entity, rather than theological leaven, appeared to be justified. See Mark D. Chapman, "The Girton Conference One Hundred Years On", *Modern Believing* 62:3 (2021), pp. 220–30.

[22] Adrian Hastings, *A History of English Christianity 1920–1985* (London: Collins, 1986), p. 261.

becomes in its turn a target for opponents? Or is it by remaining unaligned and working from within to change the climate of opinion? Even those broadly sympathetic to the attempt to recast the Christian faith in a liberal way were, at least initially, sceptical about the former option. Charles Raven, who was to become one of the leading liberal Christian thinkers of the generation after Rashdall's, reflected on his experience as a young Cambridge don in 1910:

> The Churchmen's Union was not then strong in Cambridge and hardly came into my life. From what I read of it, I concluded that it was mainly occupied in fighting over again the battles of the last century, when the question of miracles, of the Virgin Birth and the Physical Resurrection was in the centre of the field. Neither of these supposedly crucial issues has ever worried me, or seemed really important... Modernists on the whole have failed because they are at once too academic and too destructive; it is not true that "they have no gospel", but in 1910 their gospel was neither clear nor inspiring. They had not yet secured a definite place in the Church of England, were relatively few, and on the defensive; and as such their policy was to attack. For their heroism during the whole of the last half century no gratitude can be sufficient. Their efforts have saved the church. If I had seen more of them, I should have joined them earlier. As it was, I had to stand as best I could alone.[23]

---

[23] Charles E. Raven, *A Wanderer's Way* (London: Martin Hopkinson & Co., 1928), pp. 149–50. Charles Earle Raven (1885–1964): Based largely in Cambridge, as Regius Professor of Divinity from 1932 and Master of Christ's College from 1939, both held until his retirement in 1950, Raven combined theological scholarship with making significant contributions to the history of British naturalists, as well as the relationship between science and theology, as an early supporter of the work of Teilhard de Chardin. His experiences as an army chaplain during the First World War convinced him of the validity of pacifism, for which he argued consistently for the rest of his life, and his political stance was socialist.

Two years later, looking back on the conflict of the 1920s, William Temple, by this time Archbishop of York, suggested to the arch-modernist Bishop Barnes of Birmingham:

> Personally I regret the existence of a special organization of Modernists. Modernism, as you yourself describe it, is an intellectual movement leavening the whole Church, and quite indispensable to its progress or even survival. But to separate out the people specially concerned with it weakens their leavening capacity, and stiffens others in resistance.[24]

Rashdall would have agreed with much of the critique offered by Raven and Temple. In an undated lecture on "The Liberal View", likely to have been written during the First World War, he remarked:

> There is nothing which most Liberals (I imagine) shrink from more than being supposed to represent some compact body of doctrine—some cut and dried solution of the great Enigma which can be compared or contrasted with the Roman Catholic View, the High Church view, or the Evangelical view. The connecting link between Liberals is, from the nature of the case, largely negative [i.e., they are agreed in repudiating certain opinions]... liberalism represents a tendency rather than a tenet or a party.[25]

And, speaking on "Pragmatism" in 1915, there is a significant comment on one of the weaknesses of modernism:

---

[24] Temple to Barnes, January 1930, quoted in Iremonger, *William Temple, Archbishop of Canterbury*, p. 491. Barnes claimed Rashdall as a mentor: "My own philosophy is essentially that of James Ward and Hastings Rashdall. Both accepted ethical theism no less than the modern scientific outlook." Quoted in John Barnes, *Ahead of his Age: Bishop Barnes of Birmingham* (London: Collins, 1979), p. 293.

[25] Pusey House, Oxford, Rashdall MSS, HRA, B5. 12, fols 1–2.

> I have all possible sympathy with the Modernist movement, but
> I regard it as one of its great misfortunes that it should have
> allied itself to a Philosophy which does not really supply a solid
> foundation for Christianity or any other form of theistic belief.[26]

The theological warfare following the Girton conference had come at a personal cost to Rashdall. His widow, writing some 30 years later, was convinced that his ill health at this time, which was to end in his comparatively early death in 1924, was "partly caused by his persecution which he felt severely".[27]

Rashdall as a public theologian: Education and ecumenism

Reflecting ruefully on the storm created by the Girton conference, Rashdall suggested that none of it would have happened had the clergy all had theological degrees from universities. Education in general was a driving force throughout Rashdall's life, and he was committed to its development and reform. He was a strong supporter of higher education for women, becoming a member of the Council of Lady Margaret Hall in 1896; he was actively involved in the Workers' Educational Association; and he gave his public support, through letters to the press and other interventions, to forward-looking educational legislation, such as that associated with Augustine Birrell in 1906 and his old New College colleague, H. A. L. Fisher, in 1920. The education of the clergy, however, was a special concern, to which he devoted a good deal of his time and energy. Many of his Oxford pupils went on to be ordained, and he kept in touch with them on theological matters, as well as giving them more general advice. He was in demand as a lecturer and preacher at clergy

---

[26] Bodl. Lib., R. H. MSS, RH 105, 14, fol. 26, "Pragmatism", Lyceum Club, 25 February 1915.

[27] Bodl. Lib., MS Eng. Misc., c. 590, fol. 6r, Constance Rashdall to J. N. L. Myres, 31 March 1953.

gatherings and received letters from parish clergy telling him how much his books had helped them in the complexities of their ministry.

In addition to this continuous interplay, there were two institutional ventures in clergy training with which Rashdall was particularly associated. One proved successful and the other did not.

The first venture came into being at the end of the nineteenth century, when there was a concern among liberal Anglicans that there were no theological colleges which reflected their outlook, the existing ones being either catholic or evangelical. In 1897, the liberal-minded Bishop of Ripon, William Boyd Carpenter, started a small hostel to train clergy, known as Bishop's Hostel (later Bishop's College), Ripon. There was interest in starting a similar institution in Birmingham, a city which was in the midst of a controversy over ritualism at the time and where the need was felt for an anti-sacerdotal college. Rashdall was one of the principal supporters of such a move. In a letter to *The Times* in 1899 he wrote: "The real evil is the prevalence of a certain theological temper among the clergy, which is getting more and more out of harmony with the laity, and particularly of the more thoughtful and educated laity."[28] Rashdall and others formed themselves into the Midland Clergy Corporation, and the Midland Clergy College opened in Birmingham in October 1899. Like many of the smaller colleges which were springing up, it was in a large house with about half a dozen students presided over by an ordained principal. In 1901, the name was changed to Lightfoot House, in honour of the Cambridge theologian and Bishop of Durham, J. B. Lightfoot, who had ordained Rashdall.

It soon became clear that the new college was struggling to survive and was unlikely to be financially viable. It was agreed in 1906 that the colleges in Ripon and Birmingham should combine, with the ordinands from Birmingham moving to what became the Ripon Clergy College. With Rashdall's active encouragement and involvement as a governor, the college moved to the centre of Oxford in 1919 and became known as Ripon Hall. When the site was needed for the expansion of the Bodleian Library, the college moved in 1933 to Boar's Hill, on the edge of Oxford.

---

[28] *The Times*, 31 March 1899, quoted in Stephenson, *The Rise and Decline of English Modernism*, p. 80.

It remained there until 1975, when an overall decline in the number of ordination candidates led to the decision to combine it with Cuddesdon College, to form Ripon College, Cuddesdon. So two institutions founded to express different strands of Anglicanism came together. In his will, Rashdall had made a generous benefaction to Ripon Hall, as well as presenting a large number of unpublished papers to its library, and he is still commemorated in the present Ripon College by having a residential wing named after him.[29]

Rashdall's second foray into clergy training came in 1910 with his appointment by the liberal Bishop of Hereford to a residentiary canonry at Hereford Cathedral. "You will be surprised to hear that I have been offered a Canonry—and that not by a wicked, radical government but by a Bishop!", he wrote to his mother. "Before you turn over the page, guess who it is."[30] The bishop in question was John Percival, the founding headmaster of Clifton, then President of Trinity College, Oxford, where he reputedly went to recover from the exertions of establishing a new school, before becoming headmaster of Rugby (where he had William Temple, his future biographer, as a pupil). He had been at Hereford since 1895, where his radical political views and his liberal theological opinions did not particularly endear him to a largely rural and conservative diocese. But this did not deter Rashdall, who said in the same letter: … I think I should get on with him better than with any other Bishop on the bench."

The terms on which Rashdall was appointed to the canonry allowed him to retain his fellowship at New College, spending two terms in each academic year there, while residing in Hereford for five months a year. Percival's intention in appointing Rashdall was to create another small theological college under Rashdall's supervision. A small number of men—there were only ever three at any one time—would live in the

---

[29] The story of Ripon Hall and its connection with liberal theology is comprehensively discussed by Michael W. Brierley, "Ripon Hall, Henry Major and the Shaping of English Liberal Theology", in Mark D. Chapman, *Ambassadors of Christ: Commemorating 150 Years of Theological Education in Cuddesdon 1854–2004* (Aldershot: Ashgate, 2004), pp. 89–155.

[30] New Coll., PA/RAS 5/2, Rashdall to E. M. Rashdall, 2 October 1909.

Bishop's Palace. Rashdall and others would give lectures, there would be weekly essays, and a framework of prayer and devotion, making use of the cathedral. Regular meals together and the informal instruction which Rashdall provided on long walks and in other conversations would add to their formation.

Two students, both Rashdall's pupils at New College, arrived in August 1910 to start the scheme. One was Mervyn Haigh, later Bishop of Coventry and then Winchester. The other was an Australian Rhodes Scholar and England rugby international, Garnet Vere Portus. Portus was ordained in December and went back to Australia, where he soon left active church ministry to become a distinguished educationalist, while Haigh was joined in the following summer by two more students. The experiment, however, had fizzled out by the end of 1911, although Rashdall continued to have groups of students staying with him for theological instruction.

Why did it fail? It was for a combination of reasons. The idea of a one-person theological college was by now an anachronism—larger establishments were deemed to be the way forward. Nor was its establishment particularly strategic. It so happened that the one bishop in the Church of England willing to give Rashdall such a job—and it was the only episcopal appointment he received in his life—was in Hereford, which wasn't an ideal location, given the lack of sympathy many of the local clergy had with the views of Rashdall and their bishop. This confrontational attitude was exacerbated by Percival's welcoming of nonconformists to the cathedral and his subsequent appointment of B. H. Streeter, another Oxford liberal, to a canonry, as well as Rashdall's attempts to have the Athanasian Creed removed from public worship in the cathedral. The effect was to cast Hereford as a kind of fundamentalist liberal stronghold, to which it was unsafe to send prospective ordinands. This suited the demonology of both Anglo-Catholics and Evangelicals.

Another of Percival's appointments was that of Alfred Leslie Lilley, a near contemporary of Rashdall, who became a residentiary canon at Hereford in 1911 and archdeacon of Ludlow two years later. Lilley was an admirer of the Catholic modernist movement in the Roman Catholic Church and remained in close contact with some of its leading figures, such as George Tyrrell and Alfred Loisy. He was thus able to inform and encourage Rashdall's own acquaintance with this parallel movement in the Roman church.[31]

This, like many such polarizations, was a travesty of the truth. But it did not help that Rashdall's many qualities which his students at Hereford appreciated—his conscientiousness, his integrity, his humility, his sense of devotion, his commitment to the truth, his desire to build bridges to those of differing views, his impatience with ecclesiastical politics, his humour—were hidden from those who did not know him, who saw him only as a pugnacious defender of dangerous views. Mervyn Haigh shrewdly suspected that Rashdall did not, in any case, have the necessary skills to establish, lead, and develop a successful college. He did not have the administrative capacity or the willingness to play the political games which Haigh, writing as the Archbishop of Canterbury's domestic chaplain, had in abundance and knew were necessary. Haigh thought that Rashdall had C. J. Vaughan and J. B. Lightfoot in mind when training ordinands, giants of an earlier generation with their "Doves" and "Lambs".[32] That way of doing things might have worked 40 years earlier, but it was no longer possible.

—

Finally, a word about Rashdall as an ecumenist. We have already seen his ecumenical work as Dean of Carlisle and the gratitude with which it was received. In a broad sense, the whole tenor of his life was ecumenical, in that he delighted in the truth and wanted to learn from those who would help him discover more about it, regardless of their religious affiliation. He ranged across the ecclesiastical spectrum. In his work on the medieval universities, he acknowledged his debt to the great Austrian Dominican historian, Heinrich Denifle. The preface to *The Idea of Atonement* contains a tribute to another Roman Catholic scholar, Jean Rivière. Sympathetic to the work of the Catholic modernists, he

---

[31] For Lilley, see A. R. Vidler, *A Variety of Catholic Modernists* (Cambridge: Cambridge University Press, 1970), pp. 126–33.

[32] Bodl. Lib., MS Eng. misc. c. 590, fols 85–9, Haigh to Matheson, 2 November 1926.

admired what Archbishop Mignot of Albi, whom he had met in Oxford, was attempting in protecting modernists from their suppression by the Vatican and making imaginative appointments to the diocesan seminary in Albi—Rivière was a professor there.[33]

On the other hand, soon after his return to Oxford in 1888, at a meeting of the Association of Oxford Tutors, a predominantly high-church Anglican body, Rashdall spoke, against stiff opposition, in support of developing relationships with Mansfield and Manchester Colleges, the Congregationalist and Unitarian colleges recently established in Oxford.[34] He had a great respect for the work of James Martineau, Principal of Manchester College for many years, and also supported L. P. Jacks, tutor and later Principal of Manchester, in promoting *The Hibbert Journal*, which Jacks had started in 1902, becoming a member of the editorial board in 1912.[35]

Nor was his respect and admiration confined to members of his own faith. One of the most fruitful and stimulating intellectual relationships of his later life was with the Jewish scholar Claude Montefiore, effectively the founder of British Liberal Judaism, whom he met in 1913. Rashdall, who had taught Montefiore's niece at Oxford, was particularly taken with his book on *The Synoptic Gospels* (1909), which he thought gave a convincing account of the relationship of Christ's teaching to Judaism. He wrote to Montefiore:

> Your book, if I may say so, shows much more real appreciation of Jesus than the work of a good many professedly Christian—some of them even fairly orthodox—Theologians who are so obsessed with this eschatological notion that they can see nothing else

---

[33] For Mignot, see Vidler, *A Variety of Catholic Modernists*, pp. 94–105, and Louis-Pierre Sardella, *Mgr Eudoxe Irénée Mignot: 1842–1918. Un évêque français au temps du modernisme* (Paris: Cerf, 2004). Mignot came to England in 1904, on a tour which Lilley helped to arrange, visiting churchmen and academics in Oxford, London, and Cambridge.

[34] New Coll., PA/RAS, 5/2, Rashdall to E. M. Rashdall, 5 February 1890.

[35] Harris Manchester Coll., Oxford, MS. Jacks 1, fol. 77r, Rashdall to Jacks, 2 November 1912.

in the teaching of Jesus, and make Christianity consist in the following of a teacher who taught nothing of importance except an Eschatology which was after all not true.[36]

Shortly after Rashdall's death Montefiore, for his part, paid this tribute:

> I write now under the vivid sense of the terrible loss which liberal religion has sustained by the death of that great theologian ... There never was a theologian with whom (in spite of several differences) I felt in such fundamental sympathy as with him. Immensely below him in knowledge and capacity, I am yet proud to think that we looked at many things in the same sort of way.[37]

---

[36] Matheson, p. 146. It is quite possible that Montefiore's niece was "the niece of a friend" who, terrified by the experience of Rashdall's tutorials, apologized for her stupidity after one of them, to receive the reply, "I assure you I notice nothing out of the ordinary." Matheson, p. 81.

[37] Matheson, p. 147. Montefiore, who was born in the same year as Rashdall, read classics at Balliol College, where he was influenced by Benjamin Jowett and T. H. Green. Among his publications were *Judaism and St Paul* (1914) and *What a Jew Thinks about Jesus* (1935). His grandson, Alan Montefiore, was for many years a philosophy tutor at Balliol in the late twentieth century. Rashdall engaged respectfully with Montefiore's work in *Conscience and Christ*, especially at pp. 179–85.

7
Rashdall's legacy

The main purpose of this book has been to present an account of Rashdall's life and thought in the context of his time. What were the intellectual challenges he faced and how did he address them? How was his view of the world, and of God, shaped by his historical context? Such an approach is bound to reveal the complexity and inconsistency of a person's thought, particularly one, like Rashdall, who was active in many different areas, both as a scholar and as an active churchman, and who did not regard himself as constructing a tightly defined system of thought. In any case, his historical awareness had taught him that such systems rarely survived the test of time—what one century thought compelling could quickly fall out of fashion. His approach to biblical texts showed an acute awareness of their historical setting. And whenever he wrote about historical figures, from Aquinas to Jan Hus to Bishop Butler, he was careful to distinguish between those aspects of their thought which were irretrievably embedded in their time and those which could make a continuing contribution to the development of philosophy and theology.

Rashdall's life and work sheds interesting light on the preoccupations of his time; but does it have anything to say to us today? There are, after all, a number of ways in which he does not appear as an obvious role model for the twenty-first-century Church. We have noted, for example, his racism, his combative nature and sensitivity to criticism, and a curious lack of imagination or empathy when it came to considering alternative ways of seeing things. Despite his charm and his undoubted kindness and concern for those who sought his help, there is not much sign of what Keats would have called negative capability; he struggled with intellectual uncertainty and confusion, both in other people and in himself. The point was reinforced by Mervyn Haigh:

> ... sympathetic though Rashdall was in the uttermost with all who felt difficulty in believing, there was a noble decisiveness about his own mind and content. In fact, his whole life was a salutary protest alike against the moral limpness which will not commit itself and against the sentimentality into which religion too often dissolves.[1]

And H. A. Prichard observed, somewhat waspishly:

> With his colleagues he held a curious position. Though they would yield to no one in respect for his powers, it might be taken as a matter of course that however much they might be differing from one another in any discussion, Rashdall's intervention would be the signal for uniting them in a common opposition.[2]

In her entry on Rashdall in the *Oxford Dictionary of National Biography*, Jane Garnett comments on the relative neglect with which Rashdall was regarded in the years after his death. She goes on to remark that "only from the late 1980s have there been renewed flickers of interest in Rashdall among liberal intellectual churchpeople facing a new set of challenges to the sorts of approach to faith and reason which he advocated."[3] At a time when the Church can struggle to engage effectively and convincingly with the world of which it is a part, might any of those "flickers of interest" be fanned into a brighter light to show the way ahead? Or at least, to quote the poet Louis MacNeice, was Rashdall one of those who

---

[1] Bodl. Lib., MS. Eng. Misc. c. 590, fol. 89r, Haigh to P. Matheson, 2 November 1926.

[2] H. A. P[richard]., "Dr. Hastings Rashdall", *Hertford College Magazine* 13 (April 1924), p. 7.

[3] Jane Garnett, "Rashdall, Hastings", *ODNB* (Oxford: Oxford University Press, 2004).

Yet leave behind us certain frozen words
Which some day, though not certainly, may melt
And, for a moment or two, accentuate a thirst.[4]

—

The first thing Rashdall can teach us is the importance of history, both in the sense of knowledge about the past and the awareness of the ways in which societies, institutions, and systems of thought change over time, adapting to new challenges and stimuli. The history of the Church is full of examples of the adjustments made by encounters with new ways of thinking and new political realities. To take just two early instances: the encounter with Greek philosophy and with the political structures of the Roman Empire had a profound effect on the development of the Christian faith and its institutional manifestation. This has been a continuous process—the Church has had to adapt to survive; institutions which do not change will die. The notion of a Christian faith which somehow floats above the changes and chances of human history is profoundly unhistorical and non-incarnational, as is the idea of a return to some kind of golden age of "pure Christianity" or the "primitive Church", where we can be shielded from the uncertainties of the modern world. In one of his telling footnotes, William Temple states:

> ... The earth will in all probability be habitable for myriads of years yet. If Christianity is the final religion, the Church is still in its infancy. Two thousand years are as two days. The appeal to the "primitive Church" is misleading; we are the primitive Church.[5]

Rashdall continually laboured this insight in his own work, urging his readers and listeners to take the task of historical interpretation and understanding seriously, for without it any modern attempt at Christian

---

[4] Louis MacNeice, "Epitaph for Liberal Poets", in *Collected Poems* (London: Faber & Faber, 1979), p. 210. The poem was written in December 1942.
[5] William Temple, "The Church", in *Foundations* (London: Macmillan, 1913), p. 340 n. 2.

apologetic would prove to be vacuous and unconvincing. The warning is as apposite today as it was a hundred years ago: the worry is that the gulf between the Church and the modern world has become appreciably wider than it was in his day. In addition, the dawning recognition since the second half of the twentieth century that the human race now has the capacity to destroy itself, whether through nuclear warfare, climate change, or some other manufactured disaster, does not invalidate Temple's point, although it raises the theological challenge created by the abrogation by humankind of powers previously considered to be exclusively in the hands of God.

Another aspect of Rashdall's interest in history, which still has relevance today, is the importance of institutions. His stress on the medieval development of institutions such as the universities and religious orders, as the practical manifestation of movements of thought and culture, is particularly pertinent at a time such as ours, when institutions are under threat in a way that hasn't been so evident for a long time. In British society, institutions such as the monarchy, Parliament, churches, political parties, the media, schools and universities, the legal system, the police, and the financial system are no longer trusted to provide stability and continuity. It is as if the glue holding our society together is now drying out, causing its component parts to separate and fragment. People show a disinclination to join organizations unless they see a particular personal benefit in doing so. Belonging, for instance, to a church or a political party is no longer seen as something which is good in itself, a contribution to maintaining the social fabric, but as an optional extra. The language of moral obligation no longer has much currency with the large number of people who don't see the point in voting in elections: what good citizenship might look like has become increasingly hard to define in a way which doesn't betray the presuppositions of a particular interest group; there is a greater tendency to see life as an entitlement, rather than a gift. On the other hand, volunteering has grown, as people recognize a local need, whether it be helping at a food bank, or picking litter, or helping to maintain a public building. It is striking, however, that much volunteering of this kind is in effect plugging the gaps left by the decline of institutional life and agency, particularly as national and local government withdraws from providing services which were once considered to be axiomatic.

Much has changed since Rashdall's day, particularly with the revolution in communications. The internet and social media, the demand for transparency and freedom of information, mean that we are now flooded with disorganized and unedited data, which is a gift to conspiracy theorists and those who want to find evidence for a particular point of view, however unaware they might be of wider considerations. There is much commentary now on the way in which social media is dissolving the mortar of society and, ironically, making us less able to talk to each other about the things that matter. Whilst the serious-minded discussions of the Christian Social Union might appear quaint and irrelevant to our needs today, the urgency of a wide-ranging national conversation about what it is that holds us together, what it might mean to "do good", and what insights Christian faith and experience might bring to such a discussion, is still pressing. And such discussions are likely to require an institutional framework of some kind.

The consequence of a deficient understanding of history is closely connected with another of Rashdall's principal concerns: the importance of philosophy. He was writing at a time when agreement on the need for an underlying, indeed foundational, vocabulary and grammar for human discourse was taken for granted. It was not possible for people to communicate with each other at any depth unless they had a common understanding of how to make statements which were recognized to be true and trustworthy, and which would provide a reliable basis for further progress in thought. It is not that there was no disagreement about the detailed way in which the world was to be understood—Rashdall's version of personal idealism had to fight its corner against many rival theories—but there was a strong sense that the protagonists were engaged in the same enterprise. In the history of human thought, there is much that is ephemeral. This much was recognized by Rashdall's near contemporary and fellow member of the Synthetic Society, the former prime minister A. J. Balfour, who, towards the end of his life, reassured his intended biographer, Blanche Dugdale:

I don't very much care whether there is an appreciation of my philosophy. Do not worry your head with expecting permanence for philosophic thought. Not even relative permanence. All that any man's thought is, is a contribution greater or less to the stream of thought of his own time, which flows on and turns into the thought of the next generation. There is a fashion in thought—as impermanent as a fashion in dress. Something remains—goes into the stream; but it is no use to spend time in measuring the value of the fashion itself. So do not worry your head about what need be said about my philosophy.[6]

The force of Balfour's analogy, however, depends on there being a continuous stream of thought to which contributions can be made and which continues to flow. Rashdall's worry was not with the survival of philosophy as a scholarly and technical discipline with professional practitioners but with the future of general informed discourse outside the academy, in what it is now fashionable to describe as the public square. In a society, for instance, in which political life appears to be fragmented into special interest groups—some of them based on the politics of identity and nationalism—with a concentration on short-term gain over longer-term stability and co-operation, there needs to be a recovery of a coherent philosophical underpinning for political belief, which can be communicated, debated, and replenished; there needs to be a basis on which conversations can happen. The alternative is the declaration of atomized individual preferences, in which there is no real debate but only, at best, an agreement to differ, leading eventually to a scepticism or relativism, where any opinion goes. Over 40 years ago, a professor of theology at a British university wrote that he lived in daily expectation of one of his pupils telling him in an essay that mathematicians *feel* that two and two make four.[7] Since then, the privileging of feeling or emotion over reasoned discourse has grown and shows no sign of decreasing: we

---

[6] Kenneth Young, *Arthur James Balfour: The Happy Life of the Politician, Prime Minister, Statesman and Philosopher 1848–1930* (London: G. Bell & Sons, 1963), pp. 458–9.

[7] The professor was Anthony Hanson, in an opinion piece in *The Times*.

are more interested in how people feel than what they think. Rashdall's scepticism about the validity of arguments from religious experience, which have already been noted, would undoubtedly have been reinforced had he lived to see the fragmentation of reasoned defences of the faith argued from first principles.

If there is a sense in which all statements about the world and all human value-judgements are expressive of an underlying philosophical or metaphysical outlook; if we are able to recognize this and reflect on our own outlook, we are better able to engage with those around us in a joint exploration of what it is to flourish as human beings. The head of a major business school in London once told the author that he wanted to help his students to do good in their business lives. The recognition that each of the decisions they took in their working life were expressions of human value, and the challenge to reflect whether they had a consistent value system which could be resourced and sustained over time, would help them to make a greater contribution other than the simply functional and technical. It would also require them to learn more about the wider world within which their businesses functioned and with contrasting views about the value of what they were doing; to be reflective practitioners. When the training of professionals, whether businesspeople, clergy, doctors, lawyers, or others, takes place within a hermetically sealed, sterilized intellectual environment, we contribute to creating a society in which people don't really understand each other, talk past each other, and end up not bothering to make the effort, comforted instead by their own esoteric knowledge. "All professions", wrote George Bernard Shaw, "are conspiracies against the laity."[8]

This, or something like it, is the thrust of Rashdall's concern about the need for a firm philosophical basis for Christian faith. It is not to impose an intellectual straitjacket on religious belief but to recognize that there is far more to such belief than the simply affective, however significant that might be in the origin and sustenance of faith. Nor is it to prescribe or privilege a particular philosophical outlook. As Balfour suggested, there are fashions in philosophy along with everything else, and almost every philosophical stance or fashion has seen the attempt to

---

[8] G. B. Shaw, *The Doctor's Dilemma* (1906).

relate it to an articulation of Christian faith. Rashdall's work is as prone as any to the vagaries of intellectual change. There has recently been a renewal of interest in Idealist philosophers and what they might have to offer to modern thought; and to the contribution of idealism to Anglican theology. Rashdall has also attracted attention as part of a school of British ethical theorists from the late nineteenth to the mid-twentieth century, both Idealists and non-Idealists, who formed an important strand in the development of modern moral philosophy.[9] Wrong turnings have been identified as well, as was noted in the reference to Rashdall's racism. But the enterprise of connecting faith to the wider field of human thought and endeavour is part of his legacy and one that is still a challenge to us today. He has much to teach us about re-evaluating traditional ways of thinking while being open to new perspectives and avoiding absolutist stances which attempt to cancel out opposing points of view.

One particular aspect of that challenge, which may appear to be distinctly unfashionable and counter-cultural today, is to take seriously Rashdall's understanding of good and evil. At the time he was writing, and in the hundred years since then, the concepts of good and evil have been demythologized, deconstructed, and reconstructed many times. The cumulative effect of these processes has been to reduce the sense of good and evil as being objective realities: they become, rather, subjective feelings, based on a moral sense, which may be shared with others, but which falls short of objective reality. In a lecture to Cambridge undergraduates, given shortly after the publication of *The Theory of Good and Evil*, Rashdall put it like this:

> If Morality were merely a matter of feeling or emotion, actions would not be objectively right or objectively wrong; but simply

---

[9] See, e.g., W. J. Mander, *British Idealism: A History* (Oxford: Oxford University Press, 2011); *Idealist Ethics* (Oxford: Oxford University Press, 2016); Timothy Maxwell Gouldstone, *The Rise and Decline of Anglican Idealism in the Nineteenth Century* (Basingstoke: Palgrave Macmillan, 2005); Thomas Hurka (ed.), *Underivative Duty: British Moral Philosophers from Sidgwick to Ewing* (Oxford: Oxford University Press, 2011); *British Ethical Theorists from Sidgwick to Ewing* (Oxford: Oxford University Press, 2011).

right to some people, wrong to others. Hume would be right in holding the morality of an action to consist simply in the pleasure it gives to the person who contemplates it. Rightness thus becomes simply a name for the fact of social approbation. And yet surely the very heart of the affirmation which the moral consciousness makes in all of us is that right and wrong are not matters of mere subjective feeling. When I assert "this is right," I do not claim personal infallibility. I may, indeed, be wrong, as I may be wrong in my political or scientific theories. But I do mean that I think I am right; and that, if I am right, you cannot also be right when you affirm that this same action is wrong. This objective validity is the very core and centre of the idea of Duty or moral obligation. That is why it is so important to assert that moral judgements are the work of Reason, not of a supposed moral sense or any other kind of feeling. Feelings may vary in different men without any of them being in the wrong... What we mean when we talk about the existence of Duty is that things are right and wrong, no matter what you or I think about them—that the laws of Morality are quite as much independent of my personal liking and dislikings as the physical laws of Nature. That is what is meant by the "objectivity" of the moral law.[10]

Rashdall goes on to argue that to call the moral law objective is to say that it is part of the ultimate nature of things, on the same footing as physical laws. It cannot be that unless we assume that the moral law is an expression of the same mind in which physical laws originate. Thus, the idea of duty implies the idea of God, and religious belief is necessary to morality. He goes on:

> Of course I do not mean to say that, were religious belief to disappear from the world, Morality would disappear too. But I do think Morality would become quite a different thing from what it has been for the highest levels of religious thought and feeling. The best men would no doubt go on acting up to their

---

[10] *Philosophy and Religion*, pp. 71–3.

own highest ideal just as if it did possess objective validity, no matter how unable they might be to reconcile their practical with their speculative beliefs.

However:

> The only kind of objective validity which can be recognized on a purely naturalistic view of Ethics is conformity to public opinion. The tendency of all naturalistic Ethics is to make a God of public opinion. And if no other deity were recognized, such a God would assuredly not be without worshippers. And yet the strongest temptation to most of us is the temptation to follow a debased public opinion—the opinion of our age, our class, our party.[11]

In a society in which public opinion has become increasingly fragmented, the move towards subjective views of morality has become ever more pronounced, often with "values" taking the place of "truth". In a recent election for the leadership of the Conservative Party in the United Kingdom, and hence the post of prime minister, one of the candidates evidently did not think it remarkable to claim that they believed in the values of Christianity and the Church of England, although they were not a practising religious person. In a world of institutional decline and the collapse of corporate solidarity it is easy to see how discourse can be set adrift from its moorings in objective truth. A "pick-and-mix" view of the world, in which people simply agree to differ, is unlikely to lead to a constructive debate about the direction our society should take.

Rashdall is equally dismissive of views of evil which take it to be illusory, unreal, or simply a deficit in the good, rather than having real substance. In *The Theory of Good and Evil*, he formulates an ethical postulate, "the negation of Optimism, the assertion that not everything in the Universe is very good, and that the distinction between good and evil belongs to the real nature of things and not merely to appearance".[12]

---

[11] *Philosophy and Religion*, pp. 74–5.
[12] *TGE*, II, p. 244.

This is not to commit him, however, to a pessimistic world view because he believes that the world is willed by God, and:

> A rational being does not will evil except as a means to a greater good. If God be rational, we have a right to suppose that the world must contain more good than evil, or it would not be willed at all. A being who was obliged to create a world which did not seem to him good would be a blind force, as force is understood by the pure Materialist, not a rational Will... I could not regard as rational a Universe in which the good did not very greatly predominate over the evil.[13]

The conclusion to the argument is a call to engage in the moral and practical struggle against evil:

> We should... [teach] frankly that this is the best of all possible Universes, though not the best of all imaginable Universes—such Universes as we can construct in our own imagination by picturing to ourselves all the good that there is in the world without any of the evil. We may still say, if we please, that God is infinite because He is limited by nothing outside His own nature, except what He has Himself caused. We can still call Him Omnipotent in the sense that He possesses all the power there is. And in many ways such a belief is far more practically consolatory and stimulating than a belief in a God who can do all things by any means and who consequently does not need our help. In our view, we are engaged not in a sham warfare with an evil that is really good, but in a real warfare with a real evil, a struggle in which we have the ultimate power in the Universe on our side, but one in which the victory cannot be won without our help, a real struggle in which we are called upon to be literally fellow-workers with God.[14]

---

[13] *Philosophy and Religion*, p. 84.
[14] *Philosophy and Religion*, pp. 85–6.

Much has happened since Cambridge students first heard those words, and the world has changed in significant ways. Yet the challenge to human beings to play their part in salvation remains; and it may be that the wide-ranging and creative thought of that complex, passionate missionary of knowledge, Hastings Rashdall, will, despite its flaws, provide important resources to inform us and encourage us as we respond to that challenge.

> In Thought fearless, in Learning various and profound, Generous, Affectionate, Rich in humour, in his Books, in his Teaching, in his Public Duties, he brought to the service of his Age a rare passion for Virtue, Knowledge and Truth.

The words are those of H. A. L. Fisher, the distinguished historian, educator, and politician, who was an Oxford colleague of Rashdall's.[15] They are a fair summary of what Rashdall meant to those who knew him best, and what they thought future generations should know about him. That future generations should need to be reminded is an indication that Rashdall was not a major public religious figure: he was not a William Temple or a Dean Inge. His contributions were committed to the flourishing of the Church he loved, and the work he did will be continued in different ways by others. "There is no scripture against putting old wine into new bottles" was a typically mordant comment of Inge, Rashdall's former friend and colleague, and later protagonist.[16]

---

[15] The words are from Rashdall's memorial in New College. His memorial in Carlisle Cathedral has a more wordy inscription by Robert Bridges, the Poet Laureate. Bridges's involvement is not likely to have been entirely a recognition of Rashdall's public prominence: Bridges was the father-in-law of Rashdall's Oxford colleague, H. W. B. Joseph, and had become a member of the Senior Common Room at New College after being welcomed there following the destruction of his house on Boar's Hill in 1917. Although Rashdall moved to Carlisle at about the same time, it is quite possible that he would have met Bridges on return visits. Catherine Phillips, *Robert Bridges: A Biography* (Oxford: Oxford University Press, 1992), pp. 261–2.

[16] Quoted in J. A. Gere and John Sparrow, *Geoffrey Madan's Notebooks* (Oxford: Oxford University Press, 1981), p. 59.

Whether he had Rashdall in mind when he made it is not known. But if he had, it would have been an apposite comment on Rashdall's passion for presenting old truths in new ways.

Select bibliography of Rashdall's works

The complete bibliography of Rashdall's published writings, compiled by Margaret Marsh, runs to over 400 items—see Margaret Marsh, *Hastings Rashdall: Bibliography of the Published Writings* (Leysters: Modern Churchpeople's Union, 1993). It covers letters to the press, book reviews, sermons, and other occasional pieces, as well as books and articles. What is offered here is a much more modest selection of Rashdall's principal publications, including most of those referenced in the text, listed in chronological order.

John Huss (Stanhope Essay) (Oxford: T. Shrimpton & Son, 1879).
The Universities of Europe in the Middle Ages (Oxford: Clarendon Press, 1895). Revised edition, edited by F. M. Powicke and A. B. Emden, published in 1936.
Doctrine and Development (Sermons) (London: Methuen & Co., 1898).
New College, with R. S. Rait (London: F. E. Robinson & Co., 1901).
Christus in Ecclesia (Sermons) (Edinburgh: T. & T. Clark, 1904).
The Theory of Good and Evil (Oxford: Clarendon Press, 1907, second edition 1924).
Philosophy and Religion (London: Duckworth & Co., 1909).
Is Conscience an Emotion? (London: T. Fisher Unwin, 1914).
Conscience and Christ (London: Duckworth, 1916).
The Idea of Atonement in Christian Theology (Bampton Lectures for 1915) (London: Macmillan & Co., 1919).

After Rashdall's death, H. D. A. Major, Principal of Ripon Hall, together with his then colleague, F. L. Cross, collected nearly 50 of Rashdall's sermons, essays, and articles, the majority previously unpublished, in three volumes:

Principles and Precepts (Oxford: Basil Blackwell, 1927).
Ideas and Ideals (Oxford: Basil Blackwell, 1928).
God and Man (Oxford: Basil Blackwell, 1930).

Index

Abelard, Peter 39, 40, 44, 71
Anselm, St 71
Aquinas, St Thomas 39, 41-3, 44, 68, 71, 72, 98, 99, 110
Aristotle 42, 61, 67, 68
Arnold, T. 11, 15
Asquith, H. H. 26
Athanasius, St 99
Augustine of Hippo, St 71, 72, 98
Aulén, G. 80
Averroes 42

Baldwin, S. 13
Balfour, A. J. 86, 114-15, 116
Barnes, E. W. 82, 102
Barry, F. R. 81
Barth, K. 78
Berdyaev, N. 78-9
Berkeley, G. 47
Bernhardi, F. A. J. Von 92-3
Bethune-Baker, J. F. 98
Birrell, Augustine 103
Bonner, H. 7
Bosanquet, B. 48, 87, 91
Boyd Carpenter, W. 104
Bradley, F. H. 46, 48, 87
Bridges, R. 121n
Browning, R. 7, 13, 42-3
Butler, H. M. 8, 11-15, 17, 63, 64, 90
Butler, J. 2, 110

Caird, E. 20
Campbell, E. 28n
Carlisle Grammar School 29
casuistry 58-9
Christian Social Union 29, 86, 87, 89, 91, 114

Church of England Peace League 86
Churchmen's Union (later Modern Churchmen's Union) 86, 97-100
Church Reform Association 15-16
Coit, S. 94
Coleridge, S. T. 71
Collingwood, R. G. 56
Cook Wilson, J. 56, 57
Creighton, M. 25
Cuddesdon, Ripon College 105

Darwin, C. 6, 46
Darwinism 42
Davidson, R. T. 11, 13, 26, 100
Denifle, H. 107
Denney, J. 72
Dickens, C. 6, 14
Diggle, J. 27-8
Dominic, St 44
Dorrien, G. 60-1
Dugdale, B. 114
Durham, University College 18
Dyson, A. O. 63

Eliot, G. 7, 14
Emden, A. B. 36

Fisher, H. A. L. 103, 121
Francis of Assisi, St 44

Garnett, E. J. 3n, 87-8, 111
Girton Conference (1921) 97-100
Gladstone, W. E. 14
Gore, C. 11, 13, 15n, 51, 78, 84, 86, 96-7, 99
Green, T. H. 17, 20, 51, 56
Grensted, L. W. 79

Haigh, M.   106-7, 110-1
Hankey, K.   7
Hanson, A. T.   115n
Harrow School   10-15
Hastings, A.   100
Hegel, G. W. F.   47, 51
Henson, H. H.   24, 26, 91
Hereford Cathedral   20, 105-7
Holland, H. S.   51
Hügel, Baron F. von   50, 82
Hughes, T.   15
Hume, D.   61, 118
Hus, J.   17, 34-5, 110

Illingworth, J. R.   75
Inge, W. R.   20, 50, 91, 121

Jacks, L. P.   108
Jevons, F.   18
Johnson, S.   4
Joseph, H. W. B.   5, 20, 34, 121n
Jowett, B.   17, 63, 64

Kant, I.   47, 61
Keats, J.   110
King, G. L.   19

Lampeter, St David's College   18, 19
Law, W.   71
League of Nations Union   29
Lightfoot, J. B.   19, 104, 107
Lilley, A. L.   25-6, 106-7
Lincoln's Inn   21
Lloyd George, D.   6, 26
Loisy, A.   106
Lombard, Peter   71-2
Lotze, R. H.   48
Luther, M.   71

McGrath, S.   58-9
McNabb, V.   99
MacNeice, L.   111-12
Macquarrie, J.   46
McTaggart, J. M. E.   43-4, 46, 55
Makins, E.   23
Makins, H.   22-3

Makins, R.   23
Martineau, J.   99, 108
Matheson, P. E.   3n, 8, 23
Midland Clergy College (later Lightfoot House)   104
Mignot, E. I.   108
Mill, J. S.   51
Millais, J. E.   23
Milton, J.   72
Montefiore, C. G.   108-9
Moore, G. E.   43n, 55, 57

Napoleon III   15
Naval Intelligence   29
Newlands, G.   2
Newman, J. H.   14, 83

Owen, J.   18
Oxford High School   18
Oxford University:
    Balliol College   20
    Hertford College   19-20, 28
    Lady Margaret Hall   103
    Manchester College   108
    Mansfield College   108
    New College   16-17, 20-21
    St Edmund Hall   28

Percival, J.   105-6
Pfleiderer, O.   48
Plato   47
Portus, G. V.   106
Powicke, F. M.   36
Prescott, J. E.   28
Prichard, H. A.   4, 16n, 25n, 111

racism, Rashdall and   60-2
Rait, R. S.   40
Rashdall
    Agnes (HR's sister)   7, 8-10, 12, 21-2, 39, 63, 82
    Constance, née Makins (HR's wife)   7, 21-3, 31-2
    Emily (HR's mother)   7-8
    John (HR's father)   7
    Montagu (HR's brother)   7

INDEX

works:
   Doctrine and Development 64–9
   Idea of Atonement in Christian Theology 69–78
   Philosophy and Religion 117–20
   The Theory of Good and Evil 51ff.
   Universities of Europe in the Middle Ages 36–45
Raven, C. E. 101
Rawnsley, H. D. 28
Ripon Hall, Oxford 104–5
Rivière, J. 107–8
Ritschl, A. 80
Robertson, A. 18
Rowland, P. F. 36
Russell, B. 43n, 55

Schleiermacher, F. D. E. 80
Seeley, J. R. 14–15
Shaw, G. B. 116
Sidgwick, H. 51–52n, 58n, 94–6
Siedentop, L. 37n
Skelton, A. 57
Spooner, W. A. 17, 18, 20
Srinivarsan, A. 61
Streeter, B. H. 87, 106
Sturt, H. 48, 65
Summers, H. H. 30
Synthetic Society 86

Taft, W. 21n
Temple, W. 2–3, 20, 81–2, 91, 95, 102, 105, 112, 121
Tennyson, A. 7, 13, 42–3
The Group 86–7
Tout, T. F. 18, 36, 37
Treitschke, H. G. von 92
Tudhoe Grange 19
Tyerman, C. 11–12
Tyrrell, G. 106
Tyson Smith, H. 23

Vaughan, C. J. 11, 13, 107

Waldron, J. 60, 61n
Ward, Mrs H. 51
Ward, W. 83–4, 86
Webb, C. C. J. 8, 29–30, 50, 53–4, 83, 84
Westcott, B. F. 11, 71
West-Watson, C. 28
Wiles, M. F. 81n
Williams, H. H. 28
Wilson, H. 79
Workers' Educational Association 29–30, 103
Wycliffe, J. 35

Young, E. M. 12

EU GPSR Authorized Representative:

LOGOS EUROPE, 9 rue Nicolas Poussin, 17000 La Rochelle, France

contact@logoseurope.eu

www.ingramcontent.com/pod-product-compliance
Lightning Source LLC
Chambersburg PA
CBHW071450160426
43195CB00013B/2071